LEXINGTON
ROAD
TURNPIKE

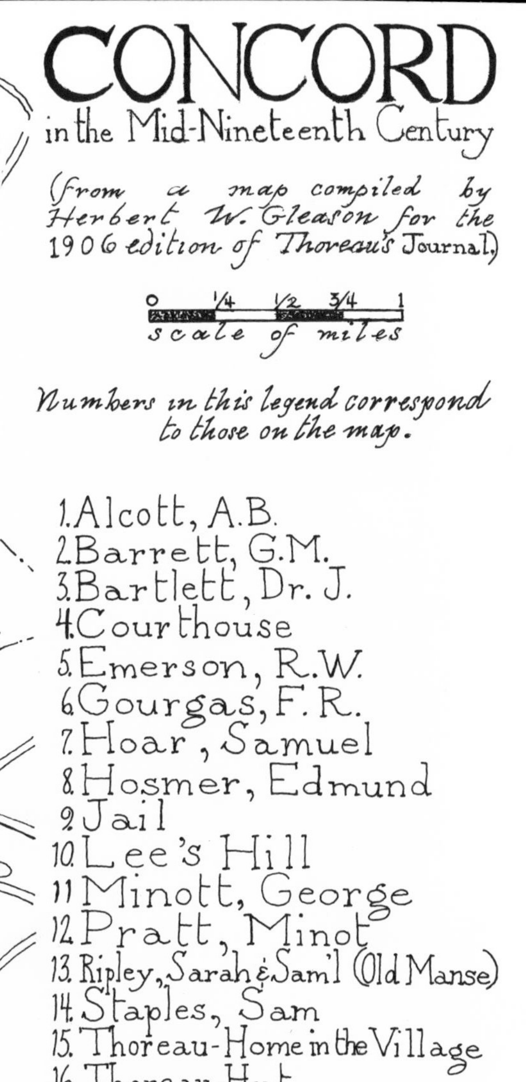
CONCORD
in the Mid-Nineteenth Century
(from a map compiled by Herbert W. Gleason for the 1906 edition of Thoreau's Journal.)
0 1/4 1/2 3/4 1
scale of miles
Numbers in this legend correspond to those on the map.
1. Alcott, A.B.
2. Barrett, G.M.
3. Bartlett, Dr. J.
4. Courthouse
5. Emerson, R.W.
6. Gourgas, F.R.
7. Hoar, Samuel
8. Hosmer, Edmund
9. Jail
10. Lee's Hill
11 Minott, George
12. Pratt, Minot
13. Ripley, Sarah & Sam'l (Old Manse)
14. Staples, Sam
15. Thoreau-Home in the Village
16. Thoreau-Hut
17. Thoreau "Texas" House
18. Town Hall
19. Unitarian Church

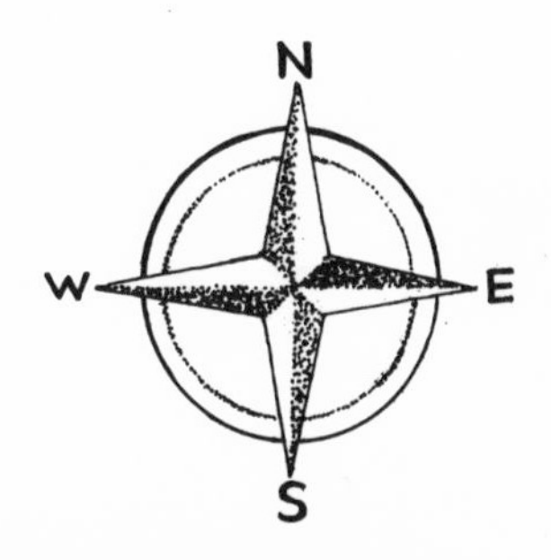
N
W
E
S

The PEOPLE *of* CONCORD

One Year in the Flowering of New England

---

by

PAUL BROOKS

Globe Pequot Press

CHESTER, CONNECTICUT

Library of Congress Cataloging-in-Publication Data

Brooks, Paul.
The People of Concord: one year in the flowering of New England/
by Paul Brooks.
p. cm.
Includes bibliographical references.
Includes index.
ISBN 0-87106-434-0
1. Concord (Mass.)—Intellectual life. 2. Transcendentalism (New England) 3. Massachusetts—Intellectual life—19th century.
I. Title.
F74.C8B79 1990
974.4'4—dc20 90-37206
CIP

Manufactured in the United States of America
First Edition/First Printing

Book and jacket design by David Ford

ACKNOWLEDGMENTS

The unique resources of the Concord Free Public Library and the cooperation of the library staff—in particular, Marcia Moss and Joyce Woodman—have made the writing of this book a pleasure. I am grateful to Claiborne Dawes for her research in certain areas and to Jeannette Cheek, David B. Little, and Judy Keyes for reading the script before publication.

Unless otherwise noted, all illustrations are reproduced by permission of the Concord Free Public Library.

NOTE

Unless stated otherwise,
all dates refer to the year 1846.

CONTENTS

PREFACE

"HISTORY," WROTE T. S. Eliot, "is a pattern of timeless moments." This book seeks to recapture, through the words and acts of a rarely articulate group of people, a decisive moment in our history—not with the perspective of a later age but as it must have appeared to them. What was it like to live in Concord, Massachusetts, during a cultural revolution that future historians would compare to the political revolution of 1775? Here was a traditional New England town, conservative in its way of life yet destined to nourish some of the most radical ideas of its time. The writers who would bring it fame were very much a part of this still-rural community; they helped to shape it, and it helped to shape them. Concord was a friendly place, where farmers mixed with intellectuals and professionals, and all spoke their minds freely. Let us take a close-up view of this little town in 1846: one frame in an ever-moving picture.

CHAPTER I

THE TIME, THE PEOPLE, AND THE PLACE

I think we escape something by living in the villages. In Concord here there is some milk of life, we are not so raving distracted with wind and dyspepsia. The mania takes a milder form. People go a-fishing, and know the taste of their meat. They cut their own whippletree in the woodlot, they know something practically of the sun and the east wind, of the underpinning and the roofing of the house, of the pan and the mixture of the soils.

—Ralph Waldo Emerson, *Journal,* 1846

Above: Concord River (Drawing by May Alcott)

THE YEAR WAS 1846. The town of Concord, lying twenty miles northwest of Boston, was more than two centuries old. The Puritans' first inland settlement, it was only five years younger than the Massachusetts Bay Colony itself. Although the original township, granted by the General Court in 1635, comprised thirty-six square miles of wilderness, this expanse had long since been reduced to manageable size as outlying districts—Acton, Bedford, Lincoln, and Carlisle—split off to form towns of their own.

Most of the area was farmland, pasture, or woodlot. But at the center lay a thriving village, just below the spot where two rivers—the sluggish Sudbury and the swifter Assabet—joined to form the Concord River, which (as Emerson wrote) "runs parallel to the village street and to which every house on that long street has a back door, which leads down through the garden to the river . . . by whose banks most of us were born."

Why the first settlers chose this spot two hundred years before is abundantly clear: the fish in the rivers, the wild game to be found in the woods and thickets, the cornfields already cultivated by the Indians, above all the tall grass meadows and fertile fields of the river valley. And in the mid-nineteenth century Concord was still a farming community.

The town was proud of its past. When in the fall of 1835 young Ralph Waldo Emerson, recently returned from Boston to his ancestral home, spoke at Concord's bicentennial celebration, he remarked on how "the agricultural favors the permanence of families. Here around me are lineal descendants of the first settlers of this town." (He himself, though born in Boston, was descended from one of Concord's principal founders, William Bulkeley.) Later in his address, Emerson recalled Concord's greatest moment in history: April 19, 1775. As he spoke, veterans of that memorable skirmish were seated beside him on the platform. "The presence of these aged men who were in arms on that day seems to bring us nearer to it."

In 1846, descendants of these founding families and of those who "fired the shot heard round the world" were still tilling the fields originally cleared and later defended by their forebears. A farming community, yes—but one in transition. The industrial revolution was in full swing. Produce from the rich soils of the Midwest was flooding eastern markets. A recently completed railroad had linked Concord with Boston; it was at once a threat to the farmers' traditional means of livelihood and a stimulus to intellectual achievement, in a period that Van Wyck Brooks described as "the flowering of New England." Names like Emerson, Alcott, Thoreau, and Hawthorne were already becoming known to the outside world. With a population of slightly over two thousand, Concord had perhaps a higher percentage of concerned and articulate inhabitants than any other small town in America. For the most part self-sufficient and highly individualistic, they saw their town and their country from differing perspectives, ranging from Emerson's abiding (though sorely tried) optimism to his close friend Henry Thoreau's conviction that his neighbors were living lives of "quiet desperation." It was a time when people's consciences were troubled, when utopian communities were seeking an alternative to growing materialism, when the drive for conquest of the continent was reaching white heat, when the issue of slavery threatened to divide the nation, when violence loomed ahead. Yet the response of this quiet little New England town was one of hope rather than despair.

By 1846 all of New England was approaching the peak of what has come to be known as the American renaissance. This was the year when Emerson delivered his great series of lectures on "Representative Men" and brought out his first book of poems; when Hawthorne published *Mosses from an Old Manse;* when Samuel Ripley, son of the legendary Ezra, returned to Concord with his brilliant wife, Sarah, to reclaim his ancestral home; when the members of the Alcott family spent their first full year at "Hillside," during which Bronson recognized "the first authentic American voice" as he listened, one winter night at Walden Pond, to Thoreau reading passages from *A Week on the Concord and Merrimack Rivers*. In nearby Cambridge, Longfellow was preparing *Evangeline* for the press, Edward Everett was installed as president of Harvard College, and the great Swiss naturalist Louis Agassiz arrived in America, soon to revolutionize Harvard's teaching of science. Farther afield, this was the year that Herman Melville published *Typee* and Whittier published *Voices of Freedom,* when the slavery issue was dividing the country, when Francis Parkman set out on the Oregon Trail and the United States went to war with Mexico.

At every level of society, Education—with a capital *E*—was seen as the key to the good life. On arriving in Boston, Agassiz was astonished to find a large group of mechanics listening earnestly to a two-hour lecture on the value of reading. Many towns besides Boston had organized lyceums (named after Aristotle's school outside Athens) for the purpose of serious discussion and instruction and hearing elevating lectures. "We are all becoming cultured up to our ears," remarked the historian William H. Prescott. *Improve-*

ment was the magic word: not only as a means of climbing the social ladder but for enrichment of life itself. The legendary factory girls in the cotton mills of Lowell are often cited as a shining example of education under benign paternalism. In view of their thirteen-hour work day, one questions the tales that they knew *Paradise Lost* by heart and discussed the English romantic poets while changing the bobbins on their looms; but they did write poems and stories for the company paper, later collected in a book called *Mind among the Spindles*. (The promise of free education, together with strict moral supervision, made it easier for the mill owners to recruit the daughters of farm families for two dollars a week, plus board.)

College education relied heavily on the classics; thorough grounding in Greek and Latin was taken for granted. (Enthusiasm for the classics included architecture, as churches and other Greek-revival buildings throughout New England still bear witness.) Knowledge of modern languages was widespread—a fact that in some instances is almost incredible by present-day standards. At the same time that American writers were creating a literature independent of Europe, young scholars were going abroad to acquaint themselves with the French utopians, with the art of France and Italy, and with the German idealistic philosophers who were having such a strong influence on the development of the transcendental movement on this side of the Atlantic. As Vernon L. Parrington points out in his *Main Currents in American Thought*, transcendentalism—now generally associated with Emerson—was a faith rather than a philosophy. Its followers "had found God for themselves before the philosophers justified them." Just as the Unitarian movement had broken away from the Calvinist concept of a sinful mortal and a wrathful God, so the new faith went a step further. "The Unitarians had pronounced human nature to be excellent; the transcendentalists pronounced it divine."

The 1840s were at once a period of expanding industry, rising commercialism, and militant nationalism and of intellectual and spiritual awakening. In the words of Edward W. Emerson (Ralph Waldo's son), "Eager study, more valiant and original writing, combinations for discussion began;* communities gathered in brave hope to make life more sensible, many-sided, higher in its plain. . . . Revelation began to appear here and there in education, religion, social and political institutions, for new questions and impulses came to the consciences of the wise, and also of the unwise, and these had to be considered and perhaps tried. Such times are uncomfortable, but had to be gone through."

In Boston and elsewhere, young men were revolting against the prosperous, complacent, materialistic society of urban America. Restless students were dropping out of college to seek truth in their own fashion. In some ways the period reminds one of the 1960s: the protest against authority, against the establishment; the opposition to an imperialistic and (as many believed) unjust war; the emphasis on self-fulfillment, on the virtues of the simple, rural life close to the soil; and the communities of like souls seeking salvation through cooperation and universal love. The doctrine of transcendentalism—which found truth in immediate perception, transcending actual experience and the learning process—cannot but remind us of the more recent interest in meditation and the spirit of Zen. So with costume: long hair, bright colors, proclaimed freedom from convention. If there

* The most famous and enduring of these groups would be the Saturday Club, founded in 1856 and still active today. Early members included, among others, Emerson, Agassiz, Lowell, Longfellow, Holmes, Whittier, and Hawthorne.

were fewer guitars, there were flutes. The very words echo across more than a century: "I want my place, my own place, my true place in the world," wrote Nathaniel Hawthorne, "my proper sphere, my thing."

Intellectually and spiritually, it was springtime in New England. The last of the ice from an earlier age was breaking up; the "main currents," so well portrayed by Parrington, were in full spate—yet with one exception: Assumptions about women's intellects, about their proper role in society, were still largely frozen in patterns of the past. Here and there, patches of open water revealed upwelling springs too powerful to be denied. Yet full acceptance of equality was generations away. The greatest tribute that the sages of Concord could pay to a woman like Margaret Fuller was to say that she had the intellect of a man.

Emerson had hoped to make Concord a haven for scholars, for creative thinkers, for people of vision who shared his faith in self-reliance and in the perfectability of the human race. That goal was never achieved. Some of those who might have helped to establish the ideal society that he visualized were diverted to more formal—and ultimately unsuccessful—utopias, such as neighboring Fruitlands and Brook Farm. Yet it was thanks to him that the Alcotts and the Hawthornes were in residence in the 1840s, that the talented and formidable Margaret Fuller was a frequent visitor, and that young poets and other of Emerson's "disciples" were giving a literary—some might say rarefied—atmosphere to the town. The strongest native voice, that of Henry Thoreau, was just beginning to be heard beyond the confines of Concord. It would gain in strength over the years and eventually penetrate every corner of the globe.

* * *

"I think I could write a poem to be called 'Concord,'" wrote Thoreau. "For argument I should have the River, the Woods, the Ponds, the Hills, the Fields, the Swamps and Meadows, the Streets and Buildings, and the Villagers. Then Morning, Noon, and Evening, Spring, Summer, Autumn, and Winter, Night, Indian Summer, and the Mountains in the Horizon."

As the year opened, Emerson's young friend and erstwhile disciple, age twenty-eight, was living in the cabin he had built on the north shore of Walden Pond. He had been there for six months, having moved in, appropriately enough, on Independence Day in 1845. Born and raised in Concord, a passionate outdoorsman, Thoreau knew every inch of the local landscape. For him, walking was a serious business. "It requires a direct dispensation from heaven to become a walker . . . ," he wrote. "I spend four hours a day at least . . . sauntering through the woods and over the hills and fields." The word *sauntering* can be misleading. Were you to ask Henry what it meant to him, he would have told you that the term was derived from those people who roamed the country in the Middle Ages, asking charity on the pretense that they were going to the Holy Land, à la Sainte Terre; they were Sainte-Terrers. For Thoreau, all land was holy. The earth, the river, and the sky supplied the raw materials in his search for truth. "How much virtue there is," he commented, "in simply seeing." For him, these daily walks through the Concord countryside were an unfailing source of excitement. To follow him in the pages of his massive journal is to get a fair impression of the topography of the town as it appeared in midcentury to its keenest observer.

One of Thoreau's favorite spots for viewing the Concord landscape at all seasons was Fairhaven Hill. Its rocky cliff overlooking the Sudbury River—just below the spot where the river broadened to form a bay or pond—was from Walden but a short walk westward: the direction in which his inner compass needle tended to point whenever he set forth. In winter the snow-covered landscape seen by moonlight from these cliffs was wholly arctic. "Fair Haven Pond is a Baffin's Bay," he wrote. But by mid-March it had become "a spring landscape, and as impossible a fortnight ago as the song of birds." From the cliffs he could look down on flocks of blackbirds settling over the swamp. In late summer the pond appeared "as through a light mist. It is the wildest scenery imaginable,—a Lake of the Woods." As evening fell, the distant lamps in a farmhouse looked like fires. "All these leaves so still, none whispering, no birds in motion,—how can I be else than still and thoughtful?"

Across the river on its west bank there ran a stretch of high ground that Henry called Conantum, after its owner, Ebenezer Conant. "He thinks that I do not visit his neighborhood more than once a year, but I go there about once a week—perhaps as often as he," wrote Thoreau. At Conantum's southern extremity rose Lee's Hill, where the Thoreau family used to go on picnics and where, it is said, one of the children narrowly escaped being born. Upstream from Lee's Bridge stretched the fertile fields of Nine Acre Corner.

Inspired though he was by these distant views, Thoreau's insatiable interest in nature took him to the wetlands that had been so vital an element in the life of the town since its founding more than two centuries earlier, when the first settlers had depended on marsh hay for their cattle as well as open fields for their corn. "Bring your sills," he wrote, "up to the very edge of the swamp!" Countless wetlands got his regular attention, the most extensive of all being the Great Meadows (the "Crane Meadows" of colonial times), a haven for wildfowl stretching northward to Carlisle.

Thoreau, while alone at Walden, did not pretend to be a hermit. His daily walks frequently took him to the village that he had known so well since childhood.

Shattuck's store (later the Colonial Inn) and the house (right) owned by Thoreau's aunts

The pattern of Concord Village in 1846 still reflected the wise planning of its founders. "The generation which planned the New England villages, divided the fields, and built the first houses," writes Samuel Eliot Morison, "seemed incapable of making anything ugly. If their laying out of homestead, village common, stone wall, road, meeting house was unconscious, the more to the credit of their instinct; for it was done in harmony with the lay of the land, the contours of valley and slope, the curve of stream and shore." Six miles square, the area originally granted to Concord was intended to accommodate new towns as population increased, with open land between town centers. The planning of the central village was anything but haphazard. A site was chosen for the meetinghouse and the village green, roads were laid out, and house lots—varying from a quarter-acre to ten acres or more—were established on the green or nearby streets. Upland and meadows were reserved for farming, grazing, and woodlots.

In 1846, Concord's original layout still remained evident. The site of the old milldam was clearly the hub; from it the spokes—the roads—extended in all directions: to Carlisle and Lowell and to Bedford, Lincoln, Lexington, Cambridge, Sudbury, and Acton. The hub itself—known as the Milldam, then as now—was largely built up, with the exception of the town common, near which stood the First Church (Unitarian), the county courthouse, the Middlesex Hotel, and two ancient cemeteries, one on either side of Mill Brook (in early days it was considered unlucky to carry a corpse across running water). Here on the Milldam were offices, shops, and some private dwellings, including that of Samuel Hoar, the town's leading citizen. At number 1, J. W. Walcott offered for sale "West India goods: Coffee, Tea, Sugars of all kinds." Close by his shop were the offices of John S. Keyes, Attorney and Counsellor at Law. The Cheap Cash Dry Goods Store advertised "Fur-Trimmed Caps." So did the Bride Store on the Milldam: "Like the Bees, prepare for a long, cold winter." And Wm. Whiting boasted of having the "Best of Sleighs that have ever been seen in this vicinity." Near Concord Bank a blacksmithing shop offered "Horse and Ox Shoeing." Concord Gun Manufactory could supply a variety of firearms, including "Fowling Pieces and Six Barrelled Pistols."

For indoor furnishings, one could buy carpets, rosewood chairs, lamps, and "Burning Fluid," as well as spectacles "warranted to suit the eyes of the most difficult." Nor were the doctors and druggists on the Milldam shy about promoting their nostrums in the weekly *Concord Freeman:* "ANOTHER LIFE SAVED! By the use of Dr. Wistan's Balsam of Wild Cherry." Clickener's Vegetable Pills were "The Grand American Purgative" (for everything). A dental surgery offered "Entire Sets of Artificial Teeth, with or without artificial gums, as the Case may require." More serious—because tragically misleading—were the supposed cures for pulmonary consumption (tuberculosis): the scourge of the period, which, by 1846, had claimed the lives of Ralph Waldo Emerson's first wife and three of his brothers.

A short distance from the village center lay the homes of many of the "lineal descendants of the first settlers" mentioned by Emerson in his bicentennial address. Everywhere were reminders of the Revolution. The home of Stedman Buttrick, whose ancestor led the charge against the redcoats on the nineteenth of April, stood on the high ground above the bridge, where the minutemen had assembled. (The annual celebration of Patriot's Day began at dawn with a seventy-five gun salute by the Concord Artillery; in 1846 it had several new fieldpieces inscribed to the memory of Major John Buttrick and Captain Isaac Davis for their valor on that occasion.) Bordering the battlefield itself stood the Old Manse, built by Emerson's grandfather, chaplain of the colonial militia, and now lived in by the Reverend Samuel Ripley and his wife, Sarah. Farther north lay the farm of Nathan Barrett, whose grandfather commanded the Concord militia during the fight at the bridge.

On the outskirts of the village, where the Cambridge Turnpike branched off from Lexington Road, lived Concord's resident best known to the world at large, Ralph Waldo Emerson.

CHAPTER II

WALDO AND LIDIAN

Voted, that the setting and conveyance by deed of part of the lot on which the East Center District School House stands, made by the Selectmen as a Committee of the town to R. Waldo Emerson on the twenty seventh day of December 1845, be ratified and confirmed by the town.

—Minutes of the January 5, 1846, Town Meeting

Above: The Emerson house (Drawing by May Alcott)

THE ACTION NOTED above and other land purchases—including Emerson's acquisition of the wooded tract by Walden Pond on which Henry Thoreau had recently built his cabin—were clear evidence, if evidence were needed, that the Emerson family was here to stay. Though born and brought up in Boston, Waldo, now in his forty-third year, had known Concord well since childhood. During his youth he had been a frequent visitor to the old Manse, built by his patriot grandfather, the Reverend William Emerson, and later presided over by the venerable Ezra Ripley, who had married William's widow and served as minister of Concord for more than sixty years. Here as a young boy Waldo acquired his abiding love for nature and the out-of-doors. As a child in the city, following the early death of his father, he had known the sharp edge of poverty; his mother, Ruth Haskins Emerson (now living with him in Concord), had struggled to make ends meet. Like many young men destined for the ministry, Waldo had supported himself by teaching school. His first wife, the young and charming Ellen Tucker, had died less than two years after their marriage. His promising career as minister of Boston's Second (Old North) Church had ended when, to the sorrow of his parishioners, Waldo felt unable to accept the orthodox view of the Lord's Supper. He was already in revolt against formalism, against the institutional authority that ran contrary to his own firm belief in self-reliance. He had come to believe that to be a good minister might in some circumstances necessitate leaving the ministry. A trip to Europe taken to restore his failing health had two lasting results: It initiated a lifelong friendship with Thomas Carlyle, whose influence on him, Thoreau, and others would be so significant, and it laid the groundwork for his first book.

His strength restored and his break with the orthodox church finally accomplished, Waldo decided in the late fall of 1834 to settle down in the village where he had spent the happiest days of his boyhood and where his roots went deep. "Hail to the quiet fields of my fathers!" he wrote in his journal. "Henceforth I design not to utter any speech, poem or book that is not entirely and peculiarly my work." For years he had been giving "hollow obeisance" to things he did not value; now he would act on his own faith. The result was a small book, written in the little upstairs study of the Old Manse, entitled *Nature*. Published anonymously in 1836, it recognized what he called the "occult relation" between human beings and all other living creatures, a concept that some readers found blasphemous. The following year he delivered the Phi Beta Kappa oration at Harvard, a speech that Oliver Wendell Holmes termed "our intellectual Declaration of Independence." And shortly thereafter he shocked the orthodox members of the Cambridge community with his Divinity School address, which was seen as a sweeping attack on the New England clergy.

By now Emerson was a highly controversial figure. "The general feeling in regard to Emerson," wrote George William Curtis, "is well expressed by John Quincy Adams in 1840: 'A young man named Ralph Waldo Emerson, a son of my once-loved friend William Emerson . . . , after failing in the avocations of a Unitarian preacher and school-master, starts a new doctrine of Transcendentalism, declares all the old revelations superannuated and worn out, and announces the approach of new revelations.' " In the summer of 1845, when Waldo had preached at Middlebury College in Vermont, the local minister, on the following Sunday, asked a special favor of God: "We beseech Thee, O Lord, to deliver us from ever hearing any more such transcendental nonsense as we have just listened to from this sacred desk." Others found Emerson both interesting and inspiring; he was in frequent demand for lectures during a period when "self-improvement" was riding high. This situation was fortunate, since the lecture platform was now his principal source of income. He did not, however, accept all invitations. When asked to speak at the New Bedford Lyceum he declined, on learning that Negroes had recently been excluded from full membership and could be seated only in the gallery. The liberal minority in the lyceum applauded his stand, and wrote to assure him of its "deepest respect for the honourable course" he had taken. They asked (and received) permission to publish his letter. Controversial though Emerson might be, his voice carried weight.

On New Year's Day in 1846, Emerson read a lecture to the Boston Lyceum on Montaigne—the fourth in a series on "Representative Men." "The search after the great man is the dream of youth," he wrote in his introduction, "and the most serious occupation of manhood." Each such man is, according to Emerson, connected with some aspect of nature, whose interpreter he is; he transcends fashion by his fidelity to universal ideas.

Eventually printed in book form, *Representative Men* would be recognized as one of Emerson's major achievements. It was, in a sense, "representative" of the man himself, who had remained faithful to his own ideas, no matter how sharply they might conflict with current views.

By now Emerson had achieved a reputation far beyond the confines of his ancestral town. But the people of Concord knew him best as a family man who had served on the school committee and taught in the Sunday school, had joined the fire company, was a prominent member of the Social Circle, and enjoyed town meetings, a man who was familiar with the family histories of his neighbors and had an extraordinary rapport with their children regardless of their ages. "Emerson was the prophet of young men," recalled one of them, "and his voice had the faculty of reaching them in the most obscure and unexpected places."

The tone of Emerson's own household was set by his second wife, an admired but less familiar figure in town. Waldo had been living in Concord for slightly more than a year when he became engaged to Lydia Jackson of Plymouth, "a person of noble character whom to see is to respect," he wrote to his brother William. (Waldo had immediately changed her name to Lidian, as more euphonious with Emerson.) "Our mother was a queenly woman," their daughter Edith would recall, "tall and graceful, and as my father desired me to notice, walked beautifully." (Indeed, "Queenie" was one of Emerson's nicknames for his wife.) Waldo had not yet found a house to his liking. "But," he wrote to Lidian, "what signifies a house, my queen! George Fox lived in a tree." Eventually, however, he located a more suitable dwelling: the Coolidge House (sometimes referred to as Coolidge Castle but called Bush by the Emerson family), on the eastern edge of the village. Northward rose the wooded Revolutionary Ridge; behind the house, meadows sloped southward to Mill Brook—a source of power in earlier days when the Milldam at the center of town served its original purpose. Emerson's bride, who turned out to be a compulsive housekeeper, immediately set about putting everything to rights. By 1846, his growing family had been living there for more than a decade.

These were the days of large families and early deaths. Waldo's family had suffered more than its share of the latter.

Ralph Waldo Emerson in 1846 (By permission of the Ralph Waldo Emerson Memorial Association and of the Houghton Library)

Of his four brothers, one had died in childhood, two had died in their twenties, and the eldest was mentally deficient. Only Waldo and William had survived. (The latter, two years Waldo's senior, was now living on Staten Island in New York.) Particularly devastating had been the loss of Waldo's younger brother Charles, a brilliant young man, generally considered the star of the family. Charles had taken over the law office of Samuel Hoar, known locally as Squire Hoar or simply as the Squire. He had become engaged to the Squire's lovely daughter Elizabeth. His presence had been a major reason for the older brother's decision to live in Concord. But in the spring of 1835, Charles had suddenly succumbed to tuberculosis. And only four years earlier Waldo and Lidian had suffered the most bitter blow of all: the loss of their first son, little

Waldo, at the age of six. This was a tragedy of which Emerson would remain keenly aware for the rest of his life.

In 1846 the household included two daughters: Ellen Tucker, seven, and Edith, five; the second son, Edward Waldo, still in infancy; and "Grandmother Emerson," Waldo's seventy-eight-year-old mother, Ruth Haskins. "It was a very happy home," recalled Edith many years later. "Our grandmother lived with us, and a sweet calm place her room always was. There each of us at the age of three came daily at ten o'clock to be taught our letters at Grandma's knee and learn to read." (Nearby lived "Aunt Lucy"—Lidian's older sister—and her two children. When Lucy's husband, an unsuccessful and apparently crooked Boston merchant, fled the country, Waldo had found her a house in Concord, and she was treated as a member of the Emerson family.)

Presiding over all with a strict attention to domestic detail was a devoted, talented, but not wholly happy woman. Lidian, a year older than Waldo, was well aware that this marriage was very different from Waldo's romantic but all-too-brief union with the young and beautiful Ellen Tucker, a decade and a half earlier. For him this second marriage was (in his words to his brother) "a very sober joy." Sensitive and intelligent, with a sharp wit and a talent for conversation, Lidian was not content merely to play the accepted role of mother and homemaker. She longed to be a writer herself. To be sure, Waldo's friends had praised her for her intellect and her spirituality. Concord, one might suppose, would be an ideal community for such a woman. Lidian's neighbors found her thoughtful and generous to those in need. But according to her daughter Ellen, she never became truly engaged in the life of the town: "She had never taken root there, she was always a sojourner, her home was Plymouth, a never-dying flame of love for Plymouth burned in her heart." Now, after eleven years, Lidian still yearned for the home of her ancestors, which Waldo had rather tactlessly dismissed as "just a sea beach." Apparently, occasional visits were not enough. On September 11, 1846, Waldo replied to an unhappy letter she had written to him from Plymouth: "I am sorry to see a little stroke of black in the end of your picture, as I thought Plymouth air and freedom and friends would scatter every cloud for three weeks at least."

If Lidian never managed to become a part of Concord, neither was she able to share her husband's philosophy of life to the extent she had once supposed. From the moment she

Lidian Emerson and Edward (By permission of the Ralph Waldo Emerson Memorial Association and of the Houghton Library)

first heard him lecture, Lidian had been convinced that she and Mr. Emerson (as she continued to call him after their marriage) were spiritual partners. Perhaps so. But as the years went by, her husband's freethinking, unconventional search for the good life had come more and more into conflict with her strictly orthodox upbringing. She made a stab at becoming a transcendentalist but failed. As Ellen later put it, "Mother never could endure philosophy." Lidian was practical, and she was strict—overacting, perhaps, the domestic role expected of her. "With the children," Ellen recalled, "Mother's rule was 'they ought never to think it possible to disobey.' " Each Sunday they had to learn a hymn; no playing was allowed on the Sabbath. Arguments between the children irritated her; "Don't bicker!" she would admonish them. Little Edward, however, learned to answer, "We aren't bickering. We are conversing on various subjects."

During much of her married life Lidian suffered—or so she believed— from ill health. From childhood she had seen herself as a martyr. Now in Concord she became obsessed with making small economies, reconstructing (with great skill) worn-out family clothing, and—to her husband's despair—indulging her passion for fresh air by opening doors and windows in the coldest weather. In 1846, the house was at last more habitable in winter. The previous year, Lidian had allowed open fires to be replaced by wood-burning stoves, and Waldo kept warm for the first time in his married life.

(Such ideas of health care were common in nineteenth-century New England, where gooseflesh was equated with godliness. Witness the Emerson's nearby neighbor, Mrs. Ellery Channing, proudly describing the regimen for her newborn baby: "We plunge her into stone cold water every morning and she comes out red as a little lobster." Ellen Emerson later commented: "I think Mother admired; I know

I did." Edward Emerson—who became a physician—recalled that many good people practiced the gospel of cold-water bathing to a dangerous degree, "breaking ice in their tubs on sharp mornings, or, in default of a temperature of 32° Fahrenheit, pumping long to get the water from the very bottom of the well." Waldo hated this ritual. He once remarked, on coming down for breakfast, "I begin to believe that the composition of water must be one part Hydrogen and three parts Conceit. Nothing so self-righteous as the morning bath—Oh, if an enemy had done this!")

Lidian had one rewarding outlet for her talents: flowers. She loved them and she grew them abundantly, including favorite roses she had brought from Plymouth. She was "the best gardener in Concord," said her neighbors. But here too her compulsion for perfection as a housekeeper asserted itself. "Put that vase in the middle of the table!" she would cry. "It ceases to be an ornament and becomes mere litter when it stands an inch or two out of position." More revealing, perhaps, was Lidian's habit of getting up in the night to rearrange books on the table, when she remembered that she had left a larger volume on top of a smaller one.

Ellen recalled that by the winter of 1845–46, "Mother felt too weak, too miserable, to keep house at all." Adding to Lidian's mental suffering was her ceaseless preoccupation with little Waldo's death four years past and with a feeling of having failed her other children. Ten days before year's end, she had written a heartbreaking letter to her husband, when she was feeling poorly and he had gone to Plymouth (presumably to deliver a lecture) without her:

> The tired child would fain have run out to play—the kind Parent knew what was better for her and put her to bed. Now do not be troubled at my egotism, dear Husband in comforting myself with this belief, in my disappointment at not going to Plymouth. . . .

> After you left the house . . . I went to bed, and have not yet risen except to have my bed made, nor taken any nourishment except cocoa & half an apple. I am better now, and hope to be about in a day or two. . . .
>
> I had a pleasant dream last night. I went into the tomb and opened Waldo's coffin—which I had a strong yearning to do. There lay the darling innocent on his side—he moved and rubbed his face on the pillow—rubbed his eyes and looked sweetly at me. I took him from his narrow bed and carried him home. He looked like his blessed self but not so large as Edie—and did not feel so heavy as Eddy. I tell you this dream because it is on me like a spell and has been all day.
>
> I hope you will write before you come and tell me every thing about the children. My waking dreams are of being some time a mother to them though your house go unswept & your bread unleavened. I must, I must! . . . I have lost Ellen's most important years. The other children are of softer material as well as of more tender years. Perhaps I can yet take care of them. Waldo is safe.

To lighten Lidian's burden, Emerson had recently hired a governess to take care of the children, a woman formerly associated with a utopian experiment in Northampton similar to Brook Farm. Named Sophia Foord (probably pronounced "Ford"), she was remembered by a friend as "a dark-skinned, pudgy-featured woman who always remained a spinster." She had, however, firm ideas on bringing up children. "We were to touch neither egg nor meat," recalled Ellen. "We were to have a pail of cold water dashed over us every morning, we were to be made active & hardy, trained to write a diary and taught sewing as well as lessons. To all this Miss Foord attended zealously, and we children all liked her."

But a governess could not take responsibility for running the household. By early spring it was clear that something would have to be done—whereupon the family members came up with an extraordinary solution to their problem: They would become boarders in their own house. A neighbor named Mrs. Marston Goodwin would take over the management of the household, bringing with her her four children, accepting as many paying boarders as there was room for.

Filling the house with strangers hardly seems a peaceful prospect for an invalid. But apparently it worked for more than a year, creating a more relaxed atmosphere, with family picnics and outings in the Concord woods arranged by Sophia and with afternoon blueberrying parties led by Henry Thoreau, driving the hay wagon full of happy boys and girls.

Ellen Emerson has left us a vivid account of these rural delights:

> Every summer, beginning about this time we had huckleberryings. Mr Thoreau would come and say he knew where they grew thick, and Father drove a carryall with Grandma & perhaps Aunt Lucy or Mrs Paine or other guests & Mr Thoreau drove the hayrigging with Miss Foord, all of us children & our Mothers and the servants. We started immediately after dinner and came home to tea. These were joyful times, Mother liked them too. Grandma, Father and Aunt Lucy never picked, they strolled about or sat in the shade, and Mr Thoreau walked hither and thither to find the best places for us, where bushes were loaded, and he & Father would cut off amazingly full ones and take [them] to Grandma. Mother always picked, and sometimes Father would put handfuls into our baskets.

For both Waldo and Henry, these would be happy interludes in a busy, creative, and sometimes disturbing year.

CHAPTER III

HILLSIDE AND WALDEN POND

What seems so fair and poetic in antiquity—almost fabulous—is realized, too, in Concord life. As poets and historians brought their work to the Grecian games, and genius wrestled there as well as strength of body, so have we seen works of kindred genius read at our Concord games, by their author, in their own Concord amphitheatre. It is virtually repeated by all ages and nations.

—Henry D. Thoreau, *Journal,* c. 1846

Above: Thoreau's cabin by Walden Pond (From the title page of *Walden,* from a drawing by Sophia Thoreau)

THE PEOPLE OF CONcord in 1846, lacking the wisdom of hindsight, could not have recognized the full stature—the impact on history—of certain neighbors who would make the town famous. Emerson was of course well known: a familiar figure ever since he had delivered the bicentennial address shortly after his arrival from Boston. On his brisk walks through the village or nearby woods, he always had a warm greeting for anyone he met on the way. "If he smiled," recalled a young admirer, "you appeared to feel the sunshine, and if he said 'Good morning,' you thought of it as a blessing." Slim, with sloping shoulders, dark brown hair, and strikingly blue eyes, Emerson would be clad in dark gray, a soft felt hat for country wear—or a black silk hat when headed for the city. In his relations with the townsfolk he had only one regret: His position inevitably set him apart. His son Edward remembered how he would "look with a longing eye at the group of village worthies exchanging dry remarks round the grocery stove, but he knew it was of no use for him to tarry, for the fact that he was scholar and clergyman would silence the oracles."

Henry Thoreau, while spending the year on the shore of Walden Pond, would often be met about town, though he boasted that he could walk all afternoon without seeing a house or crossing a highway. He took pride in wearing clothes that harmonized with the landscape: browns and greens, with an old hat in which he brought home botanical treasures. He boasted that he "could glide across the fields unperceived half a mile in front of a farmer's windows" and get nearer to wild animals in such a costume. A young friend recalled that he had "a face that you would long remember. Though short in stature, and inconspicuous in dress, you would not fail to notice him in the street, as more than ordinary." Children loved Thoreau. But to strangers—even to friends—he could occasionally be brusque. A good talker when he was in the mood, Thoreau might baffle his friends with his fondness for paradox and with his highly original way of looking at things. Yet he was one of the few visitors whom the reclusive Nathaniel Hawthorne had welcomed at the Old Manse beside the Concord River. "A singular character," noted Hawthorne in his journal, "a young man with much of the wild original nature still remaining in him. . . . He is ugly as sin, long-nosed, queer mouthed, and with uncouth and somewhat rustic—though courteous—manners. . . . But his ugliness is of an honest and agreeable fashion, and becomes him much better than beauty."

Hawthorne himself had recently—and reluctantly—left Concord for his native Salem. A shadowy figure, he had emerged from his hideout in the manse largely at night. His Concord neighbors had occasionally seen him as, avoiding the street, he walked to the post office through the woods and fields, in an old broadcloth cloak whose rusty black velvet collar hid the lower part of his face. He was well known, however, to the librarian of the Concord Athenaeum, who had been kept busy supplying him with new books. In his early forties, Hawthorne was a handsome man. He had a light, athletic build, broad shoulders, luxuriant dark brown hair and—most striking of all—"lustrous gray-blue eyes, which impressed all who knew him." (The story goes that he had once met a gypsy woman on a woodland path who stopped in astonishment: "Are you a man or an angel?") To most of Concord, however, Hawthorne had remained a man of mystery. When his *Mosses from an Old Manse* was published in early June 1846, his fellow townspeople got to know him far better than they had known him in the flesh.

As for the Alcotts, they were no strangers to the community. After the Temple School in Boston, always suspect among conventional parents, had finally foundered in 1839, its death knell sounded by Bronson's admission of a black girl, Alcott received a letter from Waldo: "Come to Concord. Our little river would run gentler and our meadows look greener to me, if such a thing could be." The following year Bronson and his wife, Abby, had rented a cottage on the farm of Edmund Hosmer. Here Henry Thoreau, an ardent admirer of Hosmer, had often come to call. Alcott, he said, "is the best-natured man I ever met. The rats and mice make their nests in him." For the Alcott family this was probably the happiest time in their lives. But in the spring of 1843 they had moved to Fruitlands in nearby Harvard, a utopian colony that Bronson and his English friend Charles Lane had founded "in hope of enjoying the pastoral life in more than pristine simplicity with a little company of men and women smitten with sentiments of the old heroism and humanity." It had collapsed within a year.

Now, in 1846, thanks once more to their patient—if sometimes exasperated—friend Emerson, the members of the Alcott family were firmly established in a house on Lexington Road, a short distance from the Emersons. (Waldo had contributed five hundred dollars toward the purchase price.) The rear windows looked out on a steep ridge, and Bronson promptly named the house Hillside, after the estate of one of his rich supporters. An early colonial farmhouse, altered over the years by a variety of owners and by now in bad need of repair, it lacked the elegance of the Emerson home. And the proximity of the heavily traveled Lexington Road was an annoyance. By late April, Bronson was complaining that "I

Bronson Alcott's sketch of Hillside, 1845

need a more adorned sphere as the show and implement of my being. The indigence of the mundane world about me affords no imagery of my thoughts and aspirations. One cannot people a world of ideas with clowns and brutes, nor create an apartment in the ideal mansion of road-dust and locust thorns.

"The petty traffic of my townspeople passes by my door; and I have not as yet been able to plant a screen of pines, larches, and spruces, to protect my eyes from the market dust, the tramp of beeves, and the roll of anxious wheels."

But Hillside was a haven all the same, and the family had immediately begun to put it to rights—Bronson working furiously indoors and out, seeking through hard manual labor to recover from the nearly fatal depression brought on by the failure of the Fruitlands experiment. "There is a martyrdom," he noted, "of the mind no less than of the body." He rationalized its failure: "You can never hurry mankind, goad them ever so fiercely. . . . No measures will avail that have their sources in mere animal will. . . . Organic changes are wrought by spiritual powers." No longer could he take refuge in his gift for schoolteaching. He still enjoyed telling moral fairy tales to children of his Concord friends and seeing their response: "I take courage on finding this faculty of touch still lively." "But now," he wrote a few days later, "I am looked upon with distrust, and while there is little hope of aiding forward mankind save by forming the young, I am prohibited from communication with these. How am I to work?"

He had thought of establishing a private school in Concord, with the Emerson's governess, Sophia Foord, as teacher. Doubtless owing to skepticism on the part of Concord parents, the school failed to materialize, but Sophia stayed on as tutor for the Alcott, Emerson, and Channing children. A nature lover, she instructed little Louisa in botany; she took them all out on picnics, berrying parties, and walks through the woods. "Many a wise lesson she gave us," recalled Louisa. "Many a flower-hunt with Thoreau for our guide . . . and endless revels where young and old played together, while illustrious faces smiled on the pretty festivities under the pines." (Unfortunately, Sophia fell in love with Thoreau, fifteen years her junior. His appalled reaction to her advances bordered on panic.)

Alcott was not the same man Concord had known in earlier days. "I have now abrogated all claims to moral and spiritual teaching," he wrote to Abby's brother, Samuel May, who had made their new home possible. "I place myself in peaceful relations to the soil, as a husbandman intent on aiding its increase, and seem no longer hostile to the powers that be." Abby herself would have preferred a fresh start in some other village, one where local gossips would not see them as an odd family that had failed once more to make a satisfactory life for themselves. But as she wrote to her brother, she felt that their new home might "help to mature a wiser and broader scheme of action than can be concocted

A. Bronson Alcott

in Mr. Alcott's celestial cogitations—Emerson will keep a rational view in sight."

Their Concord neighbors hardly knew what to make of Bronson and his family. One thing was clear: The household could not be a very happy one. The father, though obsessively concerned with shaping the character of his children, contributed nothing to their support. The mother, Abby, too proud and loyal to complain outwardly, was humiliated by having to borrow money again and again from her friends and her family, quite literally to provide the girls with enough to eat. (Schoolmates of Anna and Louisa would share their lunches with them.) Fellow townspeople who knew of the situation were concerned about the children's future, while Abby herself had to endure lectures on prudence and economy from those to whom she appealed for help. Though she felt obliged to go along with Bronson's inscrutable principles of personal conduct, she could not understand why it went against his conscience to make some attempt to support his own family. Overworked, frequently exhausted, she was still a proud, handsome, middle-aged woman with humor and spirit. But now she was almost always depressed.

Louisa May, age thirteen, had always been close to her mother; a sensitive child, she was well aware of Abby's plight. She was soon making firm resolutions that she confided to her diary:

> *March, 1846,*—I have at last got the little room I have wanted so long, and am very happy about it. It does me good to be alone, and mother has made it very pretty and neat for me. My work-basket and desk are by the window, and my closet is full of dried herbs that smell very nice. The door that opens into the garden will be very pretty in summer, and I can run off to the woods when I like.
>
> I have made a plan for my life, as I am in my teens, and no more a child. I am old for my age, and don't care much for girl's things. People think I'm wild and queer; but mother understands and helps me. I have not told any one about my plan; but I'm going to *be* good. I've made so many resolutions, and written sad notes, and cried over my sins, and it doesn't seem to do any good! Now I'm going to *work really,* for I feel a true desire to improve, and be a help and comfort, not a care and sorrow, to my dear mother.

For all her good intentions, however, Louisa was not always able to meet the strict standards of her gently dominant father. Only a month after she had made the solemn resolution above, Bronson noted in his diary: "Anna wrote a little poem in her Journal and Elizabeth studied the points and capital letters. I corrected their Journals which they wrote very faithfully. Louisa was unfaithful, and took her dinner alone."

Louisa and her mother wrote letters to each other and read each other's diaries. Abby early recognized her daughter's literary talent. On November 29, when Louisa turned fourteen, Abby presented her with a pen, along with a note of encouragement: "Lift up your soul then to meet the highest, for that alone can satisfy your great yearning nature. Your temperament is a peculiar one, and there are few who can really help you—Set about the formation of character. . . . [B]elieve me you are capable of ranking among the best." With a room of her own, Louisa had now begun to take her writing seriously. To her school friends, however, she was still the tomboy. One of them recalled "her impulsive disposition . . . fretted by the restraint and restrictions which were deemed essential to the proper girl." She was "a strange combination of kindness and perseverance, full of fun and ready wit when geniality was in ascendancy, but if the opposite, let her best friend beware."

Abby May Alcott

Abby may have found some comfort in her hopes for her talented young daughter. But she was disappointed in her expectation that the recent move to Hillside, close to her beloved

Emerson, would result in a "wiser and broader scheme of action" for the family as a whole. Although Alcott and Emerson were now nearby neighbors, their spiritual closeness had begun to deteriorate. Bronson was no longer the "majestic egoist," the fellow rebel against the materialism of the age into which they were born, the friend whom Waldo, the practical idealist, had rescued again and again from the brink of disaster. When four years earlier Waldo had suggested and financed Bronson's trip to England, Bronson had brought back to Concord two cronies whom Waldo despised—one of whom, Charles Lane, had been instrumental in the founding of Fruitlands, an act which Waldo saw as a betrayal of the intimacy he and Bronson had for so long shared.

Alcott was painfully aware of Emerson's increasing reserve. "Emerson passed the evening with me," he recorded in early April. "If the freshness of this intimacy could be renewed, as in its early youth-time!" A vain hope. More and more, Bronson's attention turned to the young man who was almost a member of the Emerson household—though currently in residence at Walden Pond.

Writing in his journal that first winter at Walden, Thoreau compared his two friends. Emerson he saw as a critic, a poet, and a philosopher, as a man whose affections and intellect were equally well developed, who was faithful and trustworthy, and who sought "to realize a divine life." Alcott, on the other hand, was a visionary, an impractical man who had limitless faith in the unseen. Alcott "habitually takes the farthest star and nebula into his scheme. When Alcott's day comes, all scales and falsehood will slough off. Everything will be in its place."

Thoreau himself was at heart a poet, and his great poem was his journal. A poet, he believed, was one "who could

Henry D. Thoreau, as sketched from memory by Edward W. Emerson

impress the winds and streams into his service, to speak for him; who nailed words to their primitive senses." Thoreau was forever living in the moment, tuned to concert pitch, alert to capture the fleeting beauty of a world whose essence is impermanence. On winter nights he would hear the booming of the ice in the pond, "restless in its bed, that would fain turn over." Occasionally, on a quiet evening he could detect the pealing of church bells from Concord and Lincoln or even farther off from Acton or Bedford, "a faint and sweet almost natural melody." Other man-made sounds reminded him that he was not so far from civilization: "The faint rattle or tinkle . . . of a carriage or team along the distant highway—the shrill whistle of the steam engine . . . sounding like the scream of a hawk sailing over some farm yard." Red or gray squirrels would awaken him at dawn, scrambling over his roof and down the sides of his cabin; flocks of chickadees would peck for crumbs at his door.

If there seemed to be no limits to Thoreau's painstaking observations and passion for fact, to his acute sense of reality, neither were there any to his powers of imagination. Here at Walden he could travel far beyond the fields and woods of Concord to the wild places of the earth and backward in time to the heroic age of myth and legend: "To cross this pond on the ice is our Davis' Straits or Baffin's Bay . . . , the men seen far over the ice . . . fishing for pickerel and moving slowly to and fro. You are uncertain whether giants or pigmies. . . . They loom up like something fabulous and incredible. Norse-like."

But the pond at Thoreau's cabin door was real, and he studied it with the trained eye of a professional surveyor. In the early spring, before the ice broke up, he measured (with extraordinary accuracy) its depth, as well as its dimensions. On March 26 he noted: "I looked out and saw that the pond was already calm and full of hope as on a summer evening—though ice was dissolved but yesterday. There seemed to be some intelligence in the pond that responded to the unseen serenity in a distant horizon. I heard a robin in the distance, the first I had heard this spring, repeating the assurance." For Henry, morning was the most memorable season of the day. On April 18 he wrote, "I get up early and bathe in the pond—that is one of the best things I do—so far the day is well spent." He complained that no one in Concord "dwells in nature;" he himself was proud to be a "self-appointed inspector of snow-storms and rainstorms. . . . Surveyor, if not of higher ways, of forest paths."

"I have endeavored to acquire strict methodical business habits," he declared. "They are indispensible." He compared himself to the owner of a shipping business, whose "vessels arrive at long and uncertain intervals." He found Walden

Pond a good port, a safe anchorage. The cargo from those voyages would, of course, become the source of *Walden:* voyages of self-discovery, of understanding man's relation to nature and man's relation to man.

"Men frequently say to me I should think you would feel lonely down there—'I should think you would want to be nearer to folks, rainy days and nights especially'. . . ," Thoreau wrote. "But after all what do we want to dwell near to?—I should say to the source of our life." Thoreau protested that he loved society "as much as most." He claimed that he "might possibly sit out the sturdiest frequenter of the bar-room, if my business called me thither." Although winter visitors were rare, he had a good deal of company during the rest of the year. "Girls and boys and young women generally seemed glad to be in the woods," he remarked. "They looked in the pond and at the flowers, and improved their time." The granddaughter of Henry's friend Edmund Hosmer recalled how "on a Sunday afternoon the children loved to go to the Walden shack. Thoreau sat at his desk, Grandfather was given a chair, while they arranged themselves along the edge of the cot bed, the youngest child still remembering that her feet couldn't quite reach the floor. If the conversation grew too abstruse or they were tired of sitting still, one by one they slipped out to amuse themselves in the woods. They might be rewarded later by a glimpse of friendly animals or Mr. Thoreau would give them a row on the pond."

Visits from schoolchildren were always welcome. In the words of a friend and former pupil: "We boys used to visit [Thoreau] on Saturday afternoons at his house by Walden and he would show us interesting things in the woods nearby. . . . He was never stern or pedantic but natural and very agreeable and friendly, but a person you would never feel inclined to fool with." The Alcott girls were, of course, favorite visitors, and these visits were never forgotten. Many years later, a former boarder in the Alcott household described boat rides on the pond, when Henry would play the flute, its music echoing over the still and beautifully clear water.

Meanwhile Henry himself made frequent visits to friends and family in the village. On February 4 he had delivered a lecture to the members of the Concord Lyceum on Thomas Carlyle, the great Scottish writer who had such a strong influence on Emerson and his contemporaries. In retrospect, that occasion seems distinguished not so much for the lecture itself as for its aftermath. During the discussion that followed, Henry had been asked not about Carlyle but about a subject that interested his audience a good deal more: Why on earth had he left his comfortable home in the village to live by himself off in the woods? To answer that question to his own satisfaction, he began writing these notes in his journal and composing a series of lectures that, eight years later, would develop into his masterwork, *Walden, or Life in the Woods.*

CHAPTER IV

FRIENDS AND NEIGHBORS

Most men are apt to exaggerate the merits of their birthplace. But I think everybody who knew the town will agree with me that there never was in the world a better example of a pure and beautiful democracy, in the highest sense of the term, than the town of Concord from 1826 to the close of the war. If there were any aristocracy, it was an aristocracy of personal worth. There was little wealth and little poverty. There were no costly dwellings and no hovels. There was no pride of wealth or of family. The richest man in town took an interest in the affairs of the poorest, as in those of a kinsman. It never occurred to the poorest that he must, for that reason, doff his hat to any man.

—George Frisbie Hoar, *Autobiography of Seventy Years*

Above: Samuel Hoar (Photography courtesy Concord Museum, Concord, Massachusetts)

SINCE COLONIAL times, Concord's population had grown steadily but slowly—somewhat more slowly than that of Massachusetts as a whole. It was notably homogeneous: Most families traced their ancestry back to a few English counties, particularly East Anglia and Kent. There were some blacks: native-born freemen and runaway slaves from the South. No Indians. One Italian. No Irish in residence—apart from those who were domestic servants, along with the builders of the railroad living in shanties near Walden Pond. In 1846 the Irish potato famine was just approaching its peak; the great wave of immigration was still a mere ripple. But Waldo Emerson already seemed concerned. That spring he confided to his journal his fear that citizens who refused to vote (in protest against government policies) would cause "the patriotic vote in the country" to be "swamped in the legion of Paddies."

The town had been—and in 1846 still was—run largely by the same families, generation after generation, but only with the advice and consent of that most democratic of political institutions, the open town meeting. "It is the consequence of this institution," Emerson had declared in his anniversary address, "that not a school-house, a public pew, a bridge, a pond, a mill-dam, hath been set up, or pulled down, or altered, or bought, or sold, without the whole population of this town having a voice in the affair. A general contentment is the result." (Emerson's audience may have detected a touch of exaggeration in this last statement.)

During 1846, Concord held six town meetings, from January 5 to December 28. Daily business was carried on by the town officers, led by the board of selectmen, whose members—then as now—were elected by vote of the town, as were the town moderator and the school committee. At the March 2 town meeting, appointments were made to various offices: Surveyors of Highways, Measurers of Wood and Bark, Surveyors of Lumber, Field Drivers, Fence Viewers, Sealers of Weights and Measures, Pound Keeper, Fire Wards, Tything Men, and Hog Reves. Many of the selectmen and other town officers in midcentury were lineal descendants of the first settlers. Names associated with early colonial times are still abundant in the town meeting records for 1846: Barrett, Buttrick, Wheeler, Hubbard, Hoar, Flint, Stow, Brown, and many more. But there is one notable exception: The chairman of the board of selectmen for that year was a relative newcomer, thirty-five years old, named Francis R. Gourgas. Born in neighboring Weston to a Swiss father and an English mother, Gourgas had attended Concord Academy, boarding with Deacon Hubbard. "He was a wild and reckless boy, a headstrong, ungovernable, and dissipated young man," recalled Judge Hoar. "Aristocratic by nature and taste, he was by profession and choice a democrat." Gourgas was also an ambitious and skillful politician who had represented Concord in the General Court, served as state senator, and held several town offices. Perhaps most important of all, he had some years earlier acquired the *Concord Freeman* and shaped it to his views, making it Middlesex County's leading Democratic newspaper. Though Gourgas was no longer its owner, the paper continued to promote his political philosophy—anti-establishment and fiercely nationalistic.

Ten years earlier, the *Freeman* had printed a series of angry articles attacking—as representing the "establishment"—an organization that did indeed embody the traditional values of the town. The Social Circle (*social* being derived from the Latin for "companion") had been founded during the late years of the American Revolution and was an outgrowth of the Committee of Public Safety. Its purpose, as stated in its constitution, was "to strengthen the social affections and disseminate useful communications among its members." The membership, limited to twenty-five, included at one time or another clergymen, doctors, lawyers, sheriffs, jailers, editors, innkeepers, bankers, tradesmen, mechanics, politicians, and—in 1846—a good representation of farmers.* Meetings were held at the houses of members, in rotation, on Tuesday evenings from October to March. Refreshments were required to "be moderate, consisting of only cyder, grogg, flip, or toddy, or either of them, as the members may desire." By 1846 the use of "ardent spirits" had been dispensed with. At the centennial celebration of the society, its historian, John S. Keyes, noted that it had included a few bachelors, "the rest married—a majority but once, a fourth part twice, a tenth part three times, and the rest so very much married that the count is not easily kept."

Emerson had been elected to membership four years after coming to live in Concord. He was well acquainted with the two men who were invited to join the club in 1846: the Reverend Barzillai Frost, minister of the First Parish for the past nine years and a man whose soporific sermons had led Waldo to seek God in the fields and woods rather than in the church, and John S. Keyes, son of the late and highly

*Edward Emerson recalled one of them, Cyrus Stow, "farmer and butcher, a neighbor of Mr. Emerson's, a solid, stately bovine man" who late in life "realized his desire of going to Washington. He reverently entered the Capitol to see the chosen great and good of the land making wise laws. He stayed one day and returned to Concord with a changed face. With lowered voice he told his neighbors that in those marble corridors were Senators and Representatives 'drinking and swearing *right before me.*' "

respected Judge John Keyes and now a young attorney with an office on the Milldam. (Another young lawyer, Ebenezer Rockwood Hoar, eldest son of the renowned Samuel Hoar, had been elected five years earlier, at the age of twenty-five, and was already launched on a brilliant career.)

The *Concord Freeman* had doubtless been correct in charging that this small, self-perpetuating group of men exerted a strong influence on town affairs. But to claim, as it did, that the Social Circle managed everything to the point where town meetings had become a pro forma routine was going a bit far. Surely it was not wholly true in a year when the anti-establishment Francis Gourgas was chairman of the Board of Selectmen!

There could scarcely be a greater contrast in background and personality than that between F. R. Gourgas and Samuel Hoar, the man who for many years had been Concord's leading citizen—in Emerson's words, "the keeper of its conscience." Known locally as the Squire, he was now sixty-eight years old, having retired to private life after a notably distinguished career at the Massachusetts Bar. Tall, erect, and slender, he had—Emerson thought—a "military air," which seems appropriate for a man who had gained his position in the community by neither intellectual brilliance nor social charm but sheer force of character. It was a family trait. The Squire's great-great-great-grandfather, John Hoar, was still remembered for his courageous defense of the "Praying Indians" (Indians in the area who had been converted to Christianity) from panic-stricken colonists during King Philip's War. Another ancestor had been president of Harvard College.

Born in Lincoln, prepared for Harvard by the Reverend Charles Stearns, Sam Hoar built up a law practice so successful that he came to be compared with Daniel Webster and Rufus Choate. "Among my earliest recollections of the administration of justice in the county of Middlesex," recalled a district judge, "was the fact that Mr. Hoar appeared to be in every case, so that apparently the only obstacle to his having a complete monopoly of the business was the impossibility of being on both sides at once." Hoar's reputation for probity, his well-known devotion to the truth, had occasionally caused confusion among juries made up largely of local farmers. Long after his retirement, stories were still told of perplexed jurors who found the law and the evidence on one side and Squire Hoar on the other. The guilt of a defendant might seem clear; but if the Squire stated in good faith that the man was innocent, who would dare contradict him?

Waldo Emerson's respect for Sam Hoar was not based on any similarity in their philosophies. "The useful and practical super-abounded in his mind," wrote Waldo. "Nobody cared to speak of thoughts or aspirations to a black-letter lawyer, who only studied to keep men out of prison, and their lands out of attachment. Had you read Swedenborg or Plotinus to him, he would have waited till you had done, and answered you out of the Revised Statutes." It was his upright character that had made Hoar the conscience of the community. On occasion this quality could be trying to his more liberal-minded neighbors, as when, with puritanical zeal, he sought to restrain unnecessary travel on the Sabbath. The story was told of an old farmer in a neighboring town who was sadly contemplating his woodland devastated by the great hurricane of 1815 and who suddenly exclaimed, "I wish this tornado had come last Sunday." "Why so?" he was asked. "Because I should have liked to see, if it came along up through Concord, whether Sam Hoar would have tried to stop it." But the ultimate accolade came from the Squire's neighbor Bronson Alcott, who, like Henry Thoreau, rejected all governmental authority: "If they will nominate Samuel Hoar for Governor, I do not know but I will recognize the State so far as to vote for him."

Sam Hoar's sense of duty—and even more, that of his strict and very serious wife, Sarah—set the tone of the household. When they were young, the children had loved to be asked to supper by the Thoreaus (Elizabeth had been a schoolmate of Henry), at whose home they found the conversation so lively and Mrs. Thoreau so amusing. Perhaps owing to their strict upbringing, the Squire's sons appeared to the family physician and friend, Dr. Josiah Bartlett, as "the three biggest rascals in Concord." Nevertheless, the doctor added, "they all seemed to have turned out pretty well." The eldest, lawyer Rockwood, was now thirty years old, married, and living next door in a newly built house on Main Street, with garden and orchard stretching down to the river. The youngest, George Frisbie—age twenty and Harvard class of 1846—was also planning a legal career.*

The other son, Edward Sherman, a hiking and boating companion of Henry Thoreau, distressed the family by leaving town briefly, when the discipline and repressive atmosphere of the household became too much to bear.

Of all the children, the one most beloved in Concord was Elizabeth, once betrothed to Waldo's brilliant younger brother, Charles. After his death she had remained single, becoming virtually a sister to Waldo and his closest confidante.

Squire Hoar was not the only one who represented the conscience of the town. Josiah Bartlett—a sturdy, hardwork-

*Rockwood would become first a judge and later U.S. attorney general under President Grant; George, a member of the U.S. Senate.

Dr. Josiah Bartlett

ing, outspoken country doctor who was married to Sarah Ripley's sister Martha—had for twenty-five years been a respected member of the Social Circle and of the Concord community at large, admired by rich and poor alike. A good friend and family doctor of the Emersons, he had recently helped to establish the town's first board of health, created largely in response to a frightening epidemic of smallpox. By July 1846, the epidemic had reached a point where a group of citizens, headed by John S. Keyes, felt they should petition the selectmen to build a town hospital. They quoted a law of the Commonwealth requiring that "when the Small pox or any other dangerous disease to the public health shall break out in any town, the board of health thereof *Shall immediately* provide Such hospital or place of acception for the Sick and infected as they Shall judge best for their accommodation and the Safety of the inhabitants." The board of selectmen, perhaps for financial reasons, declined to take any action.

Dr. Bartlett had long been concerned with another, less immediate threat to the health of the town: drunkenness. Moderate drinking had always been taken for granted, even among clergymen. "Those old-time reverend gentlemen seldom undertook to preach a sermon without their preliminary toddy," recalled the grandson of a distinguished Lincoln minister. Concord's revered Ezra Ripley had been indignant whenever rum was lacking at a funeral over which he presided; and his private practice was consistent with his public position. (His household accounts for a single month had included "1 gal. N.E. rum, 1 gal. wine, 1 gal. W.I. rum.")

Farmers worked hard and long, and many drank freely. Liquor was served at barn raisings and other festive occasions. Taverns did a brisk business, especially on election days, when candidates were wooing voters, or when the circuit court was in session. The proprietor of the Middlesex Hotel claimed that the profits of just three days in the year would pay the annual rent: the opening day of the Court of Common Pleas, the annual cattle show, and the day of the county political conventions.

All this drinking was traditional. But from what he saw as he made his daily rounds, Dr. Bartlett decided that it had gone too far. In January 1846 the town meeting confirmed a previous resolution "that in the opinion of the town, the public good does not require the licensing of any person as a retailer to sell distilled spirits of any kind in this town except for medicinal purposes and the arts." Six years earlier the Concord Total Abstinence Society had been established as an auxiliary of the Massachusetts Temperance Union. Although the society was still meeting monthly in the vestry of the First Parish Church, apparently its extreme position had limited the membership. In July the *Concord Freeman* announced the founding of the Concord True Temperance Society. The society was explicitly *not* advocating complete prohibition. There was no "taking the pledge," other than the promise to be "temperate in the use of all things." Dr. Bartlett would serve as president. A month later the *Freeman* followed up its report with an appropriate quotation from the *American Farmer*—"Harvest Drink: Mix 5 gallons of good cool water, fresh from the spring or well, half a gallon of molasses, one quart of vinegar, and 2 ounces of powdered ginger."

Dr. Bartlett's crusade had aroused the ire of the heavy drinkers. In revenge (recalled Mary Hosmer Brown), "his opponents took off the nut from a wheel, slit the curtains of his chaise, and cut off his horse's tail. The doctor rode through the streets for a long time in that style as a constant reflection on their meanness." And one morning a sign had appeared on the Middlesex stable lampooning the doctor in scurrilous verse. Emerson, passing by on his daily walk, had beaten it down with his cane.

Josiah Bartlett had one custom that must have endeared him to Concord's poor: The first day of every January, he would burn all his bills, paid and unpaid, so that his patients might start the new year with a fresh slate.

Dr. Bartlett's temperance crusade may have had limited success, but it doubtless eased the work load (seldom excessive) of another sturdy Concord citizen: Sam Staples, the town jailer. Sam was an independent, commonsense fellow, not overly concerned with the niceties of the law. "Whenever he found about the village any drunken man too overcome to take care of himself," recalled Judge Keyes, "he would collar him, drag or lead him to the jail, and lock him up for the night." In the morning Sam would send the culprit home, charging him a dollar for his lodging (a procedure that was not strictly legal but was never questioned).

The son of a blacksmith, Sam had come to Concord in 1833 at the age of twenty. He later told Thoreau that he had arrived with a dollar and three cents in his pocket and had spent the three cents for a drink at Bigelow's Tavern. Starting out as a carpenter's apprentice on the Milldam, Sam soon found a job as hostler at the livery stable opposite the Middlesex Hotel. From there it was a short step to becoming the hotel bartender and marrying the owner's daughter—with no other than Ralph Waldo Emerson presiding at the wedding. Later Sam was appointed constable and tax collector, and by 1846 he was carrying out the routine duties of town jailer, an office that would give him an enduring niche in history as the man who, that summer, put Thoreau in jail for failing to pay his taxes. They were good friends; Sam had offered to pay the tax himself, but Henry was making a point and refused. Few people in Concord, Sam felt, really knew this independent and sometimes defiant young man. It was their loss.

Staples was on equally good terms with Emerson, who in turn considered him a "most valued and respected" neighbor and member of the "village-family." Sam wondered at the number of distinguished visitors to Emerson's home, but he was not overly impressed. "Well, I suppose there's a great many things that Mr. Emerson knows that I couldn't understand; but I *know* that there's a damn sight of things that I know that he don't know anything about."

Sam Staples was not alone in feeling that few of their fellow townspeople had any idea of what Henry Thoreau was up to, living out there in the woods, or of why Emerson's high-flown, elusive doctrine of "transcendentalism" had already made his name known well beyond the confines of Concord. Horace Hosmer, an outspoken and irreverent* member of one of the oldest families in town, agreed with Sam. "The Concord people did not understand Emerson, or Thoreau, or wish to, even," Hosmer recalled many years later. "The people did not know whether Emerson and Thoreau were fluid or solid, neither did they care . . . . The misunderstanding was mutual and natural. All outside the churches and the political parties was dreamland, with a strong possibility of its being nearer to Hades than Heaven. For generations the Concord people had been instructed from the cradle to the grave to fear God and the Hoar family, to be respectable, to vote a straight ticket prepared for them by the Concord Club [presumably the Social Circle] and to pay their taxes without question or murmur."

Hosmer, who had attended the Thoreau brothers' school, virtually worshiped the whole family. Henry's father, John Thoreau, who ran the family pencil business, was "a French Gentleman rather than a Yankee . . . , French from the shrug of his shoulders to his snuff box . . . , and if you once had his confidence, a companionable person to deal with." John's neighbors found him amiable, if somewhat lacking in energy; he could spend hours happily chatting with a friend as they

*Horace Hosmer's irreverence extended to his own ancestry. "The Hosmers were English Roundheads," he said, "and were well named, for my grandfather's head was so round that he could wear his hat as well one way or another. His head was high and he was naturally religious and cruel, as a matter of course, where the love principle was absent or almost undeveloped. He married a warm hearted Scotch woman or else the tribe would have frozen to death."

sat by the stove in his pencil shop. Nor did he mind being overshadowed by his strong-minded wife, Cynthia Dunbar, who stood a head taller than he. She took an active part in the business, supervising the quality of the graphite that went into the pencils. Hosmer resented the fact that certain of the villagers thought her too talkative, something of a scold. (Ellery Channing could not stand her.) Years after her death, Hosmer spoke of her with warmth and respect. As a boy he had enjoyed the friendly atmosphere of the Thoreau household, Mrs. Thoreau's good cooking, her independence, and her forthright way of speaking. And looking back to those days, he attributed Henry's "nature-love" to his parents: "Whenever Thoreau and wife had a moment to spare they were off in the woods or fields *together*. . . . They were 20 years ahead of the times!"

Hosmer was particularly annoyed by those who saw Henry as a crank: lazy, self-centered, unwilling to work at a steady job—a young man who believed in neither the government nor the church and was generally irresponsible. (Not long before going to Walden, Henry had confirmed their opinion by accidentally setting the woods on fire during a fishing trip with Squire Hoar's son Edward. They got off lightly, doubtless owing to the position of Edward's father.) Others took a more charitable view. In 1846, when sixteen-year-old Horace Hosmer was working in a store "part restaurant, part grocery," he noticed how many customers would stop by to pick up a picnic lunch on their way to Walden for a visit with its unconventional resident. "He was visited by all sorts of people, at all hours."

But Henry did not always receive those visitors gladly. Horace recalled the experience of Benjamin Hosmer, an older brother and special chum of the Thoreau boys: "When Benj visited Henry at Walden in 1846 he walked from Bedford (some seven miles distant) and was coolly received. Henry said that 'he had no time for friendship.' " As for Horace himself, he stated that when he happened to meet Henry in the woods or fields, "I never hesitated to pass him without speaking unless I had something to ask about or to show."

Yet this apparent coldness, which Thoreau himself deplored, was anything but characteristic of his daily contact with the plain folk of Concord: the farmers, the woodchoppers, the hunters and fishermen, the rough Irishmen who had built the railroad near his cabin. He was always happy to have a chat with Alek Therien, a Canadian woodchopper with a philosophical turn of mind. "He is cast outwardly in the rudest and coarsest mould," noted Henry in his journal during his stay at Walden Pond. "I do not know whether he is as wise as Shakespeare, or as simple as a child." There was Hugh Quoil, veteran of the Battle of Waterloo, one of the Irishmen "who had gone far astray from steady habits and the village." He "lived from hand—sometimes to mouth,—though it was commonly a glass of rum that the hand carried. . . . What life he got—or what means of death—he got by ditching."

Henry, of course, had many friends among the Concord farmers, but some thought that his living off in the woods was silly and not all of them enjoyed his company. As one crusty character remarked, "If he would rather visit with woodchucks than with me and my wife, I haint nothing to say except that it is a little hard on the woodchucks."

CHAPTER V

THE "ROARING FORTIES"

One of the most dynamic phrases ever minted, "Manifest Destiny," expressed and embodied the peculiar will, optimism, disregard, and even blindness that characterized the 1840's in America.

—Bernard DeVoto, *The Year of Decision: 1846*

Above: Leaving for the war (Courtesy of the Library of Congress)

THE PEOPLE OF CONcord, thanks to their revolutionary past, possessed a particularly keen sense of history. But in 1846, not even they could be expected to grasp the full meaning of what was going on throughout the nation. Looking back near the end of the forties, the *American Review* announced that "our country has entered a new epoch in its history." To keep up with the news, the people of Concord had, of course, one lively—if somewhat biased—local paper: the *Concord Freeman,* which continued to promote the nationalistic philosophy of Francis Gourgas. In the opinion of Judge Rockwood Hoar, a conservative Whig, the paper was "an efficient political instrument, clear and forcible in style, unscrupulous and bitter, sometimes to malignity, in its partisan spirit."

Beginning with the issue of January 2, 1846, the *Freeman* almost every week printed, in addition to local items, some dramatic bit of national or international news, dealing with Texas, with the dispute with Great Britain over Oregon and—as the year wore on—with the war against Mexico. Communications with Europe were becoming closer as steam power supplemented—and on some vessels replaced—sail. Only a year earlier the first propeller-driven ship, built in England, had crossed the Atlantic. And on January 20, the paper proudly announced that the steamship *Hibernia* had made the passage from Liverpool to Boston in nineteen days (including a stopover in Halifax), bringing the latest political and economic news from England. Lord John Russell had failed to unseat Prime Minister Sir Robert Peel, who was about to win his historic fight for repeal of the notorious

Corn Laws and thus encourage free trade with America. And the stock market was up. Why should Concord readers be interested in the fluctuations of the London Stock Exchange? Because they reflected the growing conviction of the British, as well as the American people, that there could and should be a peaceful solution to the bitter dispute over possession of the Oregon Territory, which had led to a crisis in British-American relations unequaled since the end of the War of 1812.* "To borrow a figure from our neighbor Mr. Emerson," wrote the *Freeman*'s editor, "it is as important to all other men to know what Charles Francis Adams has to say [on the Oregon question] as it is to hear what the centuries have to say against the hours." (By mid-June the war cry of "fifty-four-forty or fight" had subsided and, to President Polk's chagrin, a treaty was signed setting Oregon's boundary on the forty-ninth parallel.)

Now chairman of the Concord Board of Selectmen, Gourgas was no longer the *Freeman*'s publisher, but its politics had not noticeably changed. The year's very first issue ran an editorial castigating the Whigs for opposing the admission of Texas as a state. Many New Englanders—and certainly the antislavery activists in the Boston area—saw annexation as an ominous step, sure to enlarge the Southern slave territory. What was more, the Mexican government had made clear that it would consider annexation an act of war. Nonetheless, the *Freeman* ridiculed the Whigs for their opposition: "In these times of psychological investigation, when the soul or

*The *Illustrated London News* reported on the Royal Address to Parliament of January 22, 1846: "The first striking paragraph is that containing the reference to our Oregon dispute with the United States. We gather from it a determination fully to assert the 'national honour' in the question; and it may be taken as an assurance that from the just claims of this country there will not be the slightest departure."

internal sense of things is sought after . . . it is indeed strange that it has not occurred to the Whigs of Massachusetts to inquire—why it is that this Commonwealth is continually placed in opposition to the great majority of the states of the Union on all great patriotic measures?" Massachusetts would become, the editorial continued, "the laughing stock of history."

The *Brooklyn Eagle* took the same view but went a step further. A twenty-seven-year-old editor named Walter (later shortened to Walt) Whitman, never doubting America's destiny, swept away both war scares—British and Mexican—with one characteristically grandiose gesture. Great Britain, he wrote, "can never compete with us, either in time of peace or war. . . . Mexico, though contemptible in many respects, is an enemy deserving a vigorous 'lesson.' " We can depend, he wrote, on "democracy, with its manly heart and lion strength, spurning the ligatures wherewith drivellers would bind it." The result, in Whitman's words, would be "unparalleled human happiness and rational freedom . . . to unnumbered myriads."

Many of these "drivellers" could doubtless have been found in the vicinity of Boston. Early in the spring, a petition was sent to the Massachusetts Legislature to withdraw from Congress over the Texas issue. But to the nation as a whole, the conquest of the West was clearly our "manifest destiny."* No one in Concord could be expected to visualize what this phrase meant in terms of geography. The Oregon Territory was a huge chunk of wilderness in the Far Northwest, fairly well known to fur trappers and traders

*The phrase was coined in 1845 by a journalist named John L. O'Sullivan in an editorial supporting the annexation of Texas. It was, he wrote, "our *manifest destiny* to overspread the continent allotted by Providence for the free development of our yearly multiplying millions."

and military explorers—its boundary with Canada currently in bitter dispute. Below Oregon lay "California," a part of Mexico bordered on the east by the Rocky Mountains and the independent (though Mexico still claimed sovereignty) state of Texas.

Concord readers may have received a hint of the beauty and mellow climate of the California coast from Richard Henry Dana's *Two Years before the Mast*. And soon they would have an eyewitness account of the Indian territory that lay between them and California. By late March of 1846, Francis Parkman, age twenty-three, was en route to St. Louis, the first step of his historic trip along the California and Oregon Trail. But as yet maps were vague and unreliable; much of this enormous area was unexplored. No matter. The period that had become known as the roaring forties—a time of nationalist furor and bursting expansionism—was reaching a climax under the leadership of President Polk. In 1846, Iowa became a state of the Union—the first (with the exception of Texas) west of the Mississippi—and the same year the first free homestead bill was introduced in Congress (only to be defeated by a combination of Northern Whigs and Southern Democrats). California was the promised land. Of course, it belonged to another sovereign state, the Republic of Mexico. No matter. Its manifest destiny was clearly to become a part of the United States.

Soon the editor of the *Freeman* was attacking those who "oppose the growth of our military establishment." Such views, he wrote, were sheer folly. Our country—in the early months of 1846 still at odds with Great Britain over the Oregon boundary—must be prepared to defend itself, he maintained, saying, "We have had enough cant and nonsense from peace societies and their advocates about the expense of our army and navy and the needlessness of fortifications." In April the *Freeman* quoted President Polk's message to Congress on increasing the military. It also ran the first of a series of articles on the third western expedition of that charismatic figure Lieutenant John Charles Frémont.

Frémont was already something of a popular hero. Still in his early thirties, he was the romantic pioneer par excellence, the very embodiment of the frontier spirit. The charming, able son of an émigré teacher of French and the southern belle with whom his father had eloped, Frémont began his government career as a topographical engineer. He had risen rapidly through the ranks after marrying the beautiful and strong-

John C. Frémont (From a contemporary cartoon)

willed Jessie Benton, daughter of Thomas Hart Benton, the powerful senator from Missouri. His father-in-law had given him a compelling vision of possibilities of western expansion and had sponsored two earlier explorations guided by Kit Carson and other mountain men. Young Frémont's reports of previous expeditions, published by the U.S. government, had been full of derring-do and heroic feats of endurance. In the words of historian Bernard DeVoto, they were "adventure books, charters of Manifest Destiny, texts of navigation for the uncharted sea so many dreamed of crossing." Now, week after week, Concord readers could follow Frémont's latest adventures.

In January of 1846, when his third expedition was six months out from St. Louis, Captain Frémont wrote to his wife, Jessie, from California: "Many weeks of hardships, close trials, and anxieties have tried me severely, and my hair is turning gray before its time. But all this passes, *et le bon temps viendra.*" By June he had taken credit for ordering the capture of Sonoma, north of San Francisco, which his dispatches implied was a garrisoned fortress but which (in De-Voto's words) "was a tiny cluster of adobe houses and could have been captured by Tom Sawyer and Huck Finn." The Yankee commander, citing the glories of Lexington and Concord, proclaimed the "Republic of California." From a petticoat contributed by the wife of one soldier and a chemise by another, a flag was contrived with a star in one corner, faced by a bear standing on its hind legs.*

Frémont's stirring account of what came to be known as the Bear Flag Revolt added a fresh polish to his image. Back in Concord, however, Emerson found the tone of Frémont's reports hard to take. "The stout Frémont," Emerson wrote in

* It is ironic that the California grizzly bear has long been extinct in the state whose flag it still adorns.

his journal, "in his Report of his Expedition to Oregon and California, is continually remarking on 'the group,' on 'the picture,' etc., 'which we make,' . . . this eternal vanity of *how we must look*!"

Meanwhile, the *Freeman* was printing more and more "War Intelligence" with evident satisfaction. The battles on the Rio Grande by the American forces under General Zachary Taylor, in early May, were, said the paper, "among the most gallant that have anywhere ever been fought. The army has already covered itself with glory." Lest Concord readers miss the point, the *Freeman* went on to compare these operations on the Mexican border with the battles of Napoleon—indeed with the conquest of Mexico itself by Hernando Cortés in the sixteenth century. On May 13, President Polk made an official declaration of a war that had, in fact, already begun. Concord was to raise a "Voluntary Regiment of Infantry." Volunteers, noted the *Freeman*, were to meet at Colonel Holbrook's Coffee House near the depot. Those who opposed the war, claimed the editor, were no better than the Tories during the Revolution. (Most of the volunteers in the Mexican War, some fifty thousand in number, came from Texas and the Southwest; only thirteen thousand came from the original thirteen states.)

As the war progressed, the *Freeman*'s comparison with the battles of Napoleon seemed somewhat exaggerated. The forces engaged on both sides were small. The American volunteer regiments were untrained; many of their officers were amateurs who owed their appointments to political pull. Fortunately for them, the Mexican troops were even worse off: poorly armed, poorly paid, rebellious, and eager to desert when opportunity offered. As Second Lieutenant George Meade (a young West Pointer who would win fame at Gettysburg) observed, "Well may we be grateful that we are at war with Mexico! Were it any other power, our gross follies would be punished severely."

Once the nation was officially at war, popular writers and newspaper editors inevitably evoked the proud tradition of the American Revolution, reminding readers of their heroic past. The "unsheathed sword of Washington" now rested "upon the map of the new world." Not everyone in Concord accepted the comparison. When the president declares war, Emerson complained in his journal, "democracy becomes a government of bullies tempered by editors." "The people," he wrote later, "are no worse since they invaded Mexico than they were before, only they have given their will a deed." Emerson's view of western expansion—doubtless that of many of his Concord friends—was more ambivalent than this outburst might suggest. Although he had opposed the annexation of Texas, he believed the eventual conquest of the entire West to be inevitable in the long run. War was morally wrong. But as he would later remark, "most of the great results in history are brought about by discreditable means." Even his friends at Brook Farm, that most idealistic of communities, had made the same point at far greater length—conveniently blaming the whole situation on "Providence." The editorial in their community house organ, the *Harbinger,* is surely one of the most tortuous and long-winded apologies for the war on record:

> There can be no doubt of the design being entertained by the leaders and instigators of this infamous business, to extend the "area of freedom" to the shores of California, by robbing Mexico of another large mass of her territory; and the people are prepared to execute it to the letter. In many and most aspects in which this plundering aggression is to be viewed it is monstrously iniquitous, but after all it seems to be completing a more universal design of Providence, of extending the power and intelligence of advanced civilized nations over the whole face of the earth, by penetrating into those regions

> which seem fated to immobility and breaking down the barriers to the future progress of knowledge, of the sciences and arts: and arms seem to be the only means by which this great subversive movement towards unity among nations can be accomplished. . . . In this way Providence is operating on a grand scale to accomplish its designs, making use of instrumentalities ignorant of its purposes, and incited to act by motives the very antipodes of those which the real end in view might be supposed to be connected with or grow out of.

Former Brook Farmer Nathaniel Hawthorne, on the other hand, was not concerned with these subtle distinctions. He shared the romantic view of history characteristic of the early nineteenth century—the age of Sir Walter Scott and James Fenimore Cooper. Hawthorne had complained about the difficulty of writing romances in a country "where there is no shadow, no antiquity, no mystery, no picturesque and gloomy wrong." Now young America was facing a foreign foe, a picturesque, and—for most New Englanders—mysterious people, a culture steeped in antiquity. Hawthorne saw a "chivalrous beauty" in the response of the volunteers who went to war in "the spirit of young knights." He was, in fact, reflecting the attitude of the volunteers themselves, as many of their own accounts testify. "With light hearts and bounding pulses," one of the volunteers wrote, "we left our homes . . . in quest of wild adventures in that far-famed land." William H. Prescott's *History of the Conquest of Mexico,* published in Boston in 1843, had doubtless aroused both the curiosity and the sense of romance that led young men to volunteer. Prescott himself, grandson of Colonel William Prescott of Bunker Hill fame, was coming to be known as the "American Thucydides." Though he disapproved of "the impolitic and iniquitous war in Mexico . . . mad and unprincipled," he oddly enough referred to these civilian soldiers as "pioneers of civilization"—a designation that might have surprised some of them, not to mention their officers. More realistic, perhaps, was the comment of a volunteer in Zachary Taylor's army: "What cared the youthful blood whether the war were a righteous one or not," since Mexico was a country "replete with wonder and instruction." Though the war would continue through most of the following year, by the end of 1846 the whole of California was in the hands of the North Americans.

In conquering the West, the United States had achieved (in Bernard DeVoto's words) "something that no people had ever had before, an internal, domestic empire." The preservation of this empire, this union, would soon lead to another and far greater war. Perhaps Emerson had some such foreboding when he wrote in his journal, "The United States will conquer Mexico, but it will be as the man swallows the arsenic, which brings him down in turn. Mexico will poison us." As DeVoto writes: "At some time between August and December, 1846, the Civil War had begun."

CHAPTER VI

ANTISLAVERY

Where's the man for Massachusetts?
Where's the voice to speak her free?
Where's the hand to light up bonfires
from her mountains to the sea?
Beats her Pilgrim pulse no longer?
Sits she dumb in her despair?
Has she none to break the silence?
Has she none to do and dare?

—John Greenleaf Whittier, *The Pine Tree,* 1846

Above: Antislavery broadside

The war with Mexico, sparked by the annexation of the Republic of Texas and officially declared on May 13, 1846, was tied in from the start with the issue of slavery. Forbidden under Mexican law, slaveholding had, since Texas won its independence, become a Texan institution. The acquisition of new territory large enough to create four or five more slave states obviously threatened the abolitionist cause—which had been gathering strength in Concord for the past decade. The recently founded Middlesex County Anti-Slavery Society had held its first meeting in the Concord church. A Woman's Anti-Slavery Society had been founded in Concord shortly thereafter and was soon contributing more to the abolitionist cause than any other local society in New England. Unknowingly, it would make a still-greater contribution. A founding member, Mrs. Joseph Ward, widow of a veteran of the Revolution, and her daughter Prudence had moved to Concord and made their home with Henry Thoreau's three aunts. Ardent abolitionists, they had charged the entire Thoreau family with their enthusiasm, eventually giving their cause one of its greatest spokesmen.

In the summer of 1844 Henry had found a good opportunity to show his support. Emerson, he knew, privately agreed with the abolitionists but had not yet spoken out in public. Finally, however, Emerson had been persuaded to deliver an address in the Concord Courthouse hall. But the sexton of the First Parish Church refused to ring the bell to call the meeting. His refusal was not surprising; church authorities had been very conservative on the matter of slavery, to the rage and disgust of abolitionist leaders like William Lloyd Garrison.

Garrison's outspokenness and his choice of metaphor had not endeared him to the orthodox clergy, whose churches, he proclaimed, were "cages of unclean birds, Augean stables of pollution." And although most abolitionists (and certainly Emerson) were more moderate in their views and in their language, the sexton nonetheless would have no part in calling such a meeting. Nor could anyone else be found with the courage to do so, until Henry, learning of the situation, rushed over to the church and seized the rope.

And it was Thoreau who, the following year, had defended the right of Wendell Phillips to speak at the Concord Lyceum. Phillips, a Harvard graduate now in his midthirties, was a follower of Garrison and a brilliant orator—"free of verbosity and pomposity," in the words of a contemporary. Phillips was a popular lecturer on the slavery question. But on a previous visit to Concord, his speech had offended certain of the Lyceum's conservative curators, one of whom—John Keyes—found it "vile, pernicious, and abominable." When, despite their objections, Phillips was invited to speak again, the conservative curators resigned and were replaced by Emerson, Samuel Barrett, and Thoreau; and Henry had celebrated their victory in a long and eloquent open letter published in Garrison's *Liberator*.

While at Walden, Thoreau helped to smuggle runaway slaves to his family's house, a station on the Underground Railroad. And on Saturday, August 1, 1846, the Woman's Anti-Slavery Society of Concord held, in Walden Woods, its annual commemoration of the emancipation of the slaves in the British West Indies (the same occasion for which Thoreau had rung the church bell when Emerson spoke two years earlier; this action by the British government had provided a strong stimulus to the American abolition movement). This time the group, as reported by the *Concord Freeman*, included "Rev. W. H. Channing of Boston . . . , Mr. Lewis Layden, formerly a slave, Ralph Waldo Emerson, Esq. and Rev. Mr. Skinner, the Universalist clergyman of this place. Rev. Mr. Channing, in his address, if we are correctly informed, went for the formation of a new Union and a new Constitution, and dissolution of all fellowship with slaveholding!"

A week earlier, in late July, Thoreau had made his historic gesture of going to jail rather than pay a tax to a government that condoned slavery—and that was now fighting what he considered an unjust war. The idea of such a protest was not new. Bronson Alcott and Charles Lane had both been arrested on similar grounds but had been bailed out by Squire Hoar, who feared for the town's reputation. Henry himself had taken the same stand against the local church tax, but despite his protest someone had paid the tax for him before he could be locked up. This time, however, he just managed to make it. "Thoreau was arrested early in the evening," recalled one of his early students and admirers, "while on his way to get a shoe that was being repaired preparatory to his piloting a huckleberry party on the morrow." By chance Thoreau had met his old friend Sam Staples, Concord's amiable tax collector, constable, and jailer, who had hitherto cheerfully ignored Henry's refusal to pay his tax. Sam was still reluctant to arrest him. "I'll pay your tax, Henry, if you're hard up," he said, not realizing that Thoreau's refusal to pay was "nothin' but principle." And so Thoreau spent the night in the county jail, an impressive, three-story granite building surrounded by a ten-foot brick wall, located near the Milldam.* Yet at the very last moment he had almost been foiled in making his protest. While his jailer was off on a brief

*"The large roomy jail," wrote Edmund Hosmer's granddaughter, Mary Hosmer Brown, "with its whitewashed walls was not apt to harbor any very hardened criminals."

errand, a veiled woman (doubtless Thoreau's Aunt Maria) had knocked on the door and handed Sam's daughter the tax money. Theoretically, Thoreau was now free. But as Sam remembered that evening: "I had got my boots off and was sittin' by the fire when my daughter told me, and I wasn't goin' to take the trouble to unlock after I'd got the boys all fixed for the night, so I kep' him in 'till after breakfast next mornin' and then I let him go." Thoreau, in Sam Staples's words, was "as mad as the devil" at being released. He felt that it spoiled the point he was trying to make.

Yet, as always, Thoreau made the most of the experience. "A night in prison," he later wrote, "was novel and interesting enough." His account makes it sound more like a visit to a rather well-kept poorhouse or old people's home.* When he was brought in by Sam Staples, the few prisoners were lounging around the doorway in their shirtsleeves, enjoying the evening air. "Come boys," said Sam, "it's time to lock up." Sam introduced Henry to his roommate: "a first-rate fellow and a clever man," accused of burning down a barn. Though the man claimed he never did it, he was quite content to get free board and lodging while awaiting trial. Henry, for his part, seized the opportunity to broaden his own horizons: "I pumped my fellow prisoner as dry as I could, for fear I should never see him again." At last the poor man, no doubt exhausted, managed to show Henry which bed was his and left him to blow out the light. In the morning, after a breakfast of bread and hot chocolate, Henry reluctantly accepted his free-

*A story is told of the lawyer who had called at the jail to see a man whom he had been retained to defend. The jailer told the lawyer he must come again, as the prisoner had gone huckleberrying with his children. Another story tells of the judge who, on being informed that all the prisoners had been sent to the meadow to cock hay on account of a threatened thunderstorm, immediately adjourned the court until the haying was over.

dom, while his erstwhile cellmate was sent off to make hay in a neighboring field.

In a small town, news travels swiftly. Henry's gesture elicited mixed reactions from his Concord friends. Alcott of course approved, having made similar protests himself. Immediately after Thoreau's release Bronson noted in his journal: "Had an earnest talk with Emerson dealing with civil powers and institutions, arising from Thoreau's going to jail for refusing to pay his tax. E. thought it mean and skulking, and in bad taste. I defended it on the grounds of a dignified non-compliance with the injunction of civil powers." Emerson himself apparently had second thoughts. In his journal he complained that the "rabble" in Washington (who got the United States into war with Mexico) were "Satanic," but were "really better than the snivelling opposition. . . . Mr. Webster told them how much the war cost, that was his protest, but voted the war, and sends his son to it. They calculated rightly on Mr. Webster. My friend Mr. Thoreau has gone to jail rather than pay his tax. On him they could not calculate. The Abolitionists denounce the war and give much time to it, but they pay the tax."

Thoreau himself may not have considered his aborted protest a great success. He made only a passing reference to it in *Walden*. But the jottings in his journal for this period show how deeply he felt. Outworn institutions, not people, were the object of his wrath: institutions such as the church and the state, "grim and ghostly phantoms like Moloch and Juggernaut because of the blind reverence paid to them. . . . I love mankind [but] I hate the institutions of their forefathers." His quarrel was not with his friends and neighbors: "If I will not fight—if I will not pray—if I will not be taxed—if I will not bury the unsettled prairie—my neighbor will still tolerate me and sometimes even sustain me—but not the state." Sam Staples, for instance, "as a mere man and neighbor," might be a worthy and thoughtful person, "but as the officer and tool of the state he has no more understanding or heart than his prison key or his staff." What Thoreau found so sad was "that men should voluntarily assume the character and office of brute nature." "There probably never were worse crimes committed since time began," he wrote, "than in the present Mexican War." Yet he found no single person or group to blame: "The villany is in the readiness with which men, doing outrage to their proper natures, lend themselves to perform the office of inferior and brutal ones."

While the immediate impact of Thoreau's personal rebellion may not have reached far beyond Concord, its eventual repercussions were worldwide. As the writing of *Walden* was in part stimulated by questions from fellow townspeople about Thoreau's reasons for going to live in the woods, so their curiosity about his attempt to go to jail for his principles would lead—a year and a half later—to lectures in the Concord Lyceum on "the Relation of the Individual to the State," later to be a magazine article, entitled "Resistance to Civil Government," and finally to become the world-famous essay "Civil Disobedience."* Although its implications are universal and timeless, the message of "Civil Disobedience" was directly inspired by the war with Mexico and the issue of slavery: "The standing army is only an arm of the standing government. . . . Witness the Mexican War, the work of com-

*The Concord Lyceum lecture was delivered on January 26, 1848, and repeated in February. A similar lecture had apparently been delivered in Lincoln a year earlier. Minutes of the Lincoln Lyceum for January 19, 1847, record a lecture by "Mr. Thoreau of Concord." The subject is not stated; however, immediately following this lecture, members of the lyceum chose as their next subject for debate "Is It Expedient to Obey *All Laws* whether Just or Unjust?"

paratively few individuals using the standing government as their tool; for, in the outset, the people would not have consented to this measure." Thoreau did not attempt to lay the blame elsewhere: "Practically speaking, the opponents to a reform in Massachusetts are not a hundred thousand politicians at the South, but a hundred thousand merchants and farmers here, who are more interested in commerce and agriculture than they are in humanity. . . . Those who call themselves Abolitionists should at once effectually withdraw their support, both in person and property, from the government of Massachusetts, and not wait till they have a majority of one, before they suffer the right to prevail through them. . . . Any man more right than his neighbors constitutes a majority of one already."

In his act of defiance, in his eloquent explanation of his behavior, Thoreau was addressing an immediate issue confronting the American people in the year 1846. But the impact of his words would not be confined to any era or any country. A century later, they would inspire such great leaders as Mahatma Gandhi and Martin Luther King, Jr.

When Henry made his memorable protest, he was well aware of the widening rift between New England's conservative businessmen and its liberal reformers. A salient example was the all-important cotton industry. Dependent on Southern slave labor, it pitted self-interest against conscience, the right of free enterprise against what Thoreau and the abolitionists considered to be the rights of humanity. Nationwide, this situation made strange bedfellows. "Cotton thread holds the Union together; unites John C. Calhoun and Abbott Lawrence," wrote Emerson in his journal that summer. "Patriotism [is] for holidays and summer evenings, with music and rockets, but cotton thread is the Union." The next entry extolled a man he considered a true patriot: Parker Pillsbury, an early champion of abolition and an opponent of the Mexican War. The son of a New Hampshire blacksmith and farmer, Pillsbury had studied for the ministry but soon gave up the pulpit to devote his life to social issues: antislavery, political reform, international peace, women's rights. In 1846 he was editing the *Herald of Freedom,* published in Concord, New Hampshire. "Pillsbury, whom I heard last night," wrote Emerson, "is the very gift from New Hampshire which we have long expected, a tough oak stick of a man not to be silenced or insulted or intimidated by a mob, . . . on whom neither money nor politeness nor hard words nor rotten eggs nor kicks and brickbats make the slightest impression. . . . He flings his sarcasms right and left, sparing no name or person or party or presence. The *Concord Freeman* of the last week he held in his hand (the editor was in the audience), and read the paragraph on the Mexican War from it, and then gave his own version of that fact."

Doubtless recalling the incident two years earlier when the church sexton had refused to ring the bell to announce his own speech on emancipation, Emerson concluded his private comment about Pillsbury: "What question could be more pertinent than his to the Church,—'What is the Church for, if, whenever there is any moral evil to be grappled with, as Intemperance, or Slavery, or War, there needs to be originated an entirely new instrumentality?' "

If the church was unwilling to grapple with the issue of slavery, not all its supporters were so timid. Only recently Squire Hoar, by then in his late sixties, had willingly accepted a difficult—and in retrospect a dangerous—mission. At the request of the governor of Massachusetts and the state legislature, he had sailed to Charleston, South Carolina, to test the constitutionality of a shocking piece of new legislation: a state law under which free Negroes serving as seamen on vessels touching at South Carolina ports could be seized, jailed, and (if not bailed out) sold into slavery. On arrival, Hoar was warned that he might be lynched. When he refused to abandon his mission, a mob surrounded his hotel and forced him to return to his ship, an episode that caused a wave of indignation throughout New England.

Men like Sam Hoar belied the distorted image that the commercial interests in New England sought to impose on the opponents of slavery, eager as these businessmen were to separate themselves from any liberal views that might offend their Southern customers. Tory newspapers railed against the leaders of the antislavery movement as atheists, wild-eyed radicals, enemies of the state. These were unlikely terms to apply to the Quaker poet John Greenleaf Whittier or to Theodore Parker, Wendell Phillips, Charles Sumner, James Russell Lowell, or—of all people—Concord's Squire Hoar.

CHAPTER VII

BROOK FARM: CONCORD'S UTOPIAN NEIGHBOR

The forties probably gave rise to more movements of reform than any other decade in our history; they marked the last struggle of the liberal spirit of the eighteenth century in conflict with the rising forces of exploitation.

—F. O. Matthiessen, *American Renaissance*

Above. Brook Farm as it appeared in 1897.

WHILE HENRY THOreau was defying a state that he considered immoral and while abolitionists were fighting for social justice, other dedicated liberals were seeking by different means the "unparalleled human happiness and rational freedom" that Walt Whitman thought would result from the conquest of Mexico. The goal was not acquisition of new land to be explored and exploited but rather the reform of society by means of new communities, based on a different concept of the good life. Along with the current passion for learning, there had developed a heightened social awareness. Optimism knew no bounds. In 1845 Robert Owen, the British reformer and founder of New Harmony, Indiana, had summoned a "World Convention to Emancipate the Human Race from Ignorance, Poverty, Division, Sin and Misery." More and more young men and women were in revolt against the complacent, materialistic world of urban America. Religious leaders were questioning ancient dogmas, as they looked not only to a future heaven but to a fulfilling life here on earth. Emerson was but one of many ministers who felt that they could best serve mankind outside the confines of the established church. Rural communities were being organized as places where social rank was banished, where the dignity of manual labor was recognized, and where one took for granted the divinity of both mankind and nature. By the 1840s, some thirty or forty such would-be utopias had been founded. One of the most promising and most carefully planned (in contrast, for example, to Alcott and Lane's abortive Fruitlands), as well as the one most closely linked to the people of Concord, was

Brook Farm in West Roxbury, some five miles southwest of Boston. By 1846 it had survived more than four years of gallant struggle against difficult odds. But that year would see its dramatic demise.

Brook Farm had been founded in 1841 by Dr. George Ripley, a friend and contemporary of Emerson and a relation of the latter's step-grandfather, the legendary Ezra Ripley. Like Emerson, George Ripley had resigned his pulpit in Boston to find his fulfillment, his duty to society, outside the church. From "the Great Awakener," the Unitarian leader William Ellery Channing, Ripley received the inspiration for an ideal community in which manual labor and intellectual activity would be united, in which "the members, instead of preying on one another, and seeking to put one another down . . . should live together as brothers seeking one another's elevation and spiritual growth."

For this awesome undertaking, George Ripley and his wife, Sophia Dana, chose a dairy farm of 170 acres bordering the Charles River, which they already knew and loved from summer vacations. Sophia expressed her delight with the "birds and trees, sloping green hills and hay fields as far as the eye can reach—and a brook clear running," which sang them to sleep "with its quiet tune" and "chanted its morning song to the rising sun"—and which, in due time, would give a name to their noble experiment. (The farmhouse itself was aptly named the Hive.) Unfortunately, the rich green mantle that Sophia so admired covered a rather poor and gravelly soil: adequate for a family garden but far from ideal for supporting the number of people that she and George had in mind. Perhaps dedication to their cause would make up for the lack of topsoil. Aware of the practical problems that these inexperienced husbandmen would face, Ripley had been acquiring a shelfful of books on agriculture, ranging from the recently published eight-volume *Treatise on Landscape Gardening and Rural Agriculture* by America's first great landscape gardener, Andrew Jackson Downing, to Samuel L. Dana's *A Muck Manual for Farmers.*

The founders of Brook Farm, however lofty their ideals, were practical people. They began by drawing up a constitution, or "Articles of Agreement," for what they named the Institute for Agriculture and Education. (The second purpose is significant. The Brook Farm school was an essential—and perhaps the most successful—part of the whole enterprise; it included an infant school, a primary school, and a six-year preparatory course for those destined for college. Studies were elective, and every pupil was to spend a daily hour or two in manual labor.) The association was financed by the sale of one or more shares of stock, at five hundred dollars apiece.

From the start, the connection with Concord was close. The principles on which the enterprise was based had been thrashed out at meetings of the so-called Transcendental Club. Present and future Concordians, such as farmer Minot Pratt, the great schoolteacher George P. Bradford, and—of all people—Nathaniel Hawthorne, were among the founders. Hawthorne, who had (in the words of his publisher, James T. Fields) "a physical affinity with solitude," apparently joined Brook Farm under a misconception. He was no crusader for communal living or social reform; rather, he saw here an opportunity to write undisturbed for half the day, after earning his keep by farm work the other half. A vain hope. As he wrote to his fiancée, Sophia Peabody, "After a hard day's work in the gold mine [the manure pile] my soul obstinately refuses to be poured out on paper. . . . A man's soul may be buried and perish under a dung-heap or a furrow in the field, just as well as under a pile of money." Within six months he had left, having grown "sick to death of playing at philanthropy and progress." Yet others discovered the community life and rural tasks to be quite congenial. Notable among them were George William Curtis and his elder brother Burrill, who were only eighteen and twenty years of age, respectively, when they joined the community. Handsome and courtly in their manners, they appeared to the female residents like "young Greek gods," according to Edith R. Curtis—though it was also argued that Burrill, whose hair fell in "irregular curls" to his shoulders, was more "Raphaelesque." They charmed the company on picnics and at evening musicals but never neglected their share of the work. As for George Ripley himself, he especially enjoyed milking, which he found conducive to contemplation, "particularly when the cow's tail is looped up behind"—a fine illustration of the principle he had expressed somewhat more formally when he founded this community in which "thought would preside over the operations of labor, and labor would contribute to the expansion of thought."

Ripley could be lighthearted about his experiment, but he had suffered a bitter disappointment at the very outset. After long hesitation, Emerson had politely but firmly refused to join him. "It is quite time," his friend had written, "that I made an answer to your proposition that I should venture into your new community. . . . I have decided not to join it, yet very slowly, and I may almost say with penitence." Emerson found the plan "noble and generous." But it was not for him. To Margaret Fuller (who was closely associated with Brook Farm but never a member) he wrote, "At the name of a Society all my repulsions play, all my quills rise and sharpen." As he noted in his journal: "I do not wish to remove from my present prison to a prison a little larger. . . . To join this body would be to traverse all my long trumpeted theory that one man is a counterpoise to a city."

Waldo also had more mundane reasons for refusing to take part in this idealistic venture. Was he physically fit for such strenuous manual labor? Was the enterprise itself financially sound? He had consulted his neighbor, Edmund Hosmer, Concord's most successful farmer. Hosmer had his doubts about the very idea of "gentlemen farmers"; they were not only inexperienced, they were too honest. "No large property," he told Waldo, "can ever be made by honest farming." What was needed was a shrewd foreman who would "sell the produce without any scrupulous inquiry on the part of the employer as to his methods." Not precisely what the Reverend George Ripley had in mind when he left the pulpit to serve the cause of honest living and brotherly love.

Brook Farm had to get along without Emerson. But ties between Concord and West Roxbury remained close, with much visiting back and forth. In addition to George and Sophia Ripley, Waldo had a number of friends among these utopians. He enjoyed giving informal talks at the Hive or the Grape Vine. Recalled Hosmer's granddaughter: "He was always happy and serene, never hilarious, smiled much, laughed seldom, but his beautiful face and wonderfully illuminating smile made him very attractive." And Hosmer himself, despite his skepticism about the farm members' survival, took pleasure in attending the occasional picnic or garden party that leavened their labor. Later on, several Brook Farmers would move to Concord, among them the talented and charming Curtis brothers, who boarded with Captain Nathan Barrett, with the Hosmers, and later with Minot Pratt and who helped Thoreau to build his cabin at Walden Pond. There was also the gifted schoolteacher George P. Bradford, Brook Farm's "instructor in Belles Lettres," who came back to town to tutor the Emerson children. And—most conspicuously—there was the prima donna of Brook Farm, the enchanting

Almira Barlow, whose departure was not wholly voluntary. She had been less interested in the affairs of the community as a whole than in certain attractive young men she found there. She made advances to, among others, a shy, religiously troubled mystic named Isaac Hecker (later to become well known as the founder of the Paulist Fathers). Hecker fled to the austerity of Fruitlands. The directors of Brook Farm, encouraged by the other women in the colony, sent Almira packing. The ever-gallant George William Curtis met the stage that brought her and her three young sons to Concord, and Curtis found them a suitable dwelling. As he wrote to a former recipient of Almira's perfumed notes at Brook Farm, "Her house is a small neat cottage between the graveyards . . . at the corner where we go to Sleepy Hollow. Out of all windows except one, she is reminded of mortality. She seems very much as usual and quite cheerful. . . . She might be much more economical than she is, but I understand her feelings and have respect for them."

Brook Farm was some two years old when it became indoctrinated—one might better say infected—with the bizarre doctrines of the French social philosopher Charles Fourier. Fourierism was all the rage among American utopians, and there was growing pressure to form Brook Farm into a "phalanx," as the unit in his system was called. Oddly for a former minister, George Ripley himself had become a convert. The Frenchman's theory of "attractive industry," which advocated a more congenial and varied work program, with tasks suitable to the individual worker, was enlightened, if not practical. But his ideas on sex were, in Emerson's words, "very French indeed." In love as in industry, Fourier maintained, men and women should follow their natural impulses. Whereas God governed the universe by "attraction"—by pleasure, not restraint—abstinence from pleasure was a very great sin. In the future, Fourier shrewdly predicted, divorce would be more readily accepted and would increase with the economic independence of women. But he didn't stop there. Even the heavenly bodies, like humans, he argued, yearn for their mates; they have passions and "aromas" that enable them to copulate at a distance. The aurora borealis, he said, betokens that the Earth is holding out lonely hands of love to Venus.

Alas for Brook Farm, the music of the spheres turned out to be anything but a love song. Although disciples of Charles Fourier, such as journalist Arthur Brisbane, who had been proselytizing Dr. Ripley from the start, wisely played down the free-love aspects of the movement, this was not the sort of society the original founders and their friends had in mind. Hawthorne, now married and living in the Old Manse, compared Fourier's phalanx to an ant colony. Emerson feared for the morals of the younger generation. And attacks on Fourierism by the New York press were causing something of a scandal. Nonetheless, the Brook Farmers adopted a new constitution and, although almost bankrupt, set to work constructing a large central building, called a "phalanstery," to accommodate the increased membership they anticipated. Unfortunately, it would never be occupied.

Monday evening, March 2, 1846. Work on the phalanstery, delayed by lack of funds (it had cost seven thousand dollars), was nearing completion. Accommodation for some 150 people should be ready by fall. A dance was in progress at the Hive. "Fire! The phalanstery!" someone shouted. In no time flames had spread throughout the unfinished building. George Ripley's sister Marianne, accepting this as God's will, was struck by the wild beauty of the scene, "glorious beyond description. How grand when this immense heavy column of smoke first rose up to heaven! . . . It was spangled with fiery sparks, and tinged with glowing colors, ever rolling and wreathing, solemnly and gracefully up—up."

Marianne and many others faced this dramatic blow from heaven (probably caused by a spark from a defective chimney on unplastered lath) with remarkable serenity—even with a sort of exaltation. The struggle to finish this ambitious structure, which would have greatly enlarged and altered the community, was now over. Perhaps that was all to the good; the group members would continue as before. But in fact it meant the end of the Brook Farm experiment. The community never recovered and was officially dissolved early in the new year.

Few Brook Farmers had so close and lasting connections with Concord as the colony's scholarly and beloved schoolteacher, George P. Bradford. Younger brother of Emerson's aunt Sarah Bradford Ripley, George had been an intimate friend of Waldo since childhood, and it was he who had later introduced Bronson Alcott to the Emerson family. George was an outdoor companion of Henry Thoreau, who considered him a first-rate naturalist; to Hawthorne he was "the rarest man in the world"—so rare that Nathaniel, almost unbelievably, invited Bradford to board with him and Sophia in their private Eden, the Old Manse—an offer that he wisely declined.

Those lucky enough to study under George Bradford at Brook Farm never forgot the experience. "I learned easier and faster with him than any other teacher I was ever under," recalled Frederick Pratt. George William Curtis, Bradford's pupil at Brook Farm and later in Concord, appreciated his qualities as a scholar but even more "the social sympathy and tenderness of feeling that brought him into intimate personal relations which time could not touch." Emerson, four years Bradford's senior, had noted in his journal, "I can better

George P. Bradford

converse with G. B. than with any other." (In later years, he described Bradford to Thomas Carlyle as "one of the three companions I find in Concord.")*

For all that, Waldo's lifelong friend was an elusive character: unworldly, eccentric, shy, self-deprecatory, given to periods of melancholy, and unable to stick with any job for long. He traveled frequently to Europe. "He was always active, even to apparent restlessness," recalled Curtis, "not from

*The other two companions were undoubtedly Sarah Ripley and Elizabeth Hoar.

nervous excitement, but from fullness of life and sympathy. You might think of a humming-bird darting from flower to flower, of a honey-bee happy in a garden." Bradford's sister Sarah (who was fourteen years his senior), having prepared him for Harvard and striven patiently to build up his self-confidence, was more succinct: "He would not be happy in heaven unless he could see his way out." His nearest approach to a profession was teaching school: in Plymouth (Lidian Emerson's native town), in Concord, and in other New England communities, though never in one place for long. And despite his shyness, he managed to speak on the lyceum circuit. Characteristically, he began one lecture: "Ladies and gentlemen, I wish that I could improve these humble performances and render them less unworthy of your attention."

Bradford remained a scholarly bachelor: diffident in manner, almost childlike in his freshness of feeling and frankness of speech. His appearance was as unworldly as his character. "His features," recalled Maud Howe, a Brook Farm pupil, "suggested an affectionate sheep. . . . His clothes were unlike any I have ever seen." The people of Concord loved him. Emerson had more than one reason to treasure his friendship: An expert gardener and a former business partner of a Plymouth horticulturist, Bradford tended the flowers and shrubs at Coolidge Castle whenever opportunity offered. He had left Brook Farm when it became indoctrinated with the ideas of Charles Fourier, so alien to his own view of life. Now, in 1846, he was back in Concord, tending his own vegetable garden, surely the finest in town.

George Bradford had unknowingly influenced the course of Emerson's life when, in 1834, he invited his friend to deliver a lecture in Plymouth. Lydia Jackson was in the audience and was charmed by the speaker. She had never met Emerson but had been greatly impressed by a sermon she had chanced to hear on a visit to Boston. Soon after the lecture in Plymouth, he was asked back to preach. He seemed to be expressing her own thoughts. According to family tradition, Lydia subsequently had a vision of herself dressed as a bride, walking down the stairs of the Winslow house in Plymouth with Emerson at her side. Be that as it may, a close friendship developed during later visits, encouraged by Bradford and other mutual friends. When Waldo wrote proposing marriage she was amazed, but after a serious discussion she gave her consent. As noted earlier, Waldo considered their relationship "a very sober joy." But George was doubtless pleased with what he had inadvertently brought about.

No one has recorded fonder memories of this unique Concord character than Edmund Hosmer's granddaughter, Mary Hosmer Brown. Let her have the last word:

> "There was one man whom I met at various houses, sometimes at our own, and I loved to catch up with him and share for a bit his walk, he was so unassumingly wise. Sometimes I would offer, as the guests were leaving, to help him on with his overcoat, which offer he always refused. But he never forgot, when the coat was on, to stop and shake hands and wish me a cordial good night. He never made his name so well known in the world at large, but he was as typical a character in his way as any of Concord's more noted men. You felt instinctively that he was a superior soul, but his wisdom was so enshrined by his modesty, he seemed so contented in his own sphere, that you never thought to ask, had he discovered this or that, or was he famous in any way, but only left his presence deeply thankful that in this restless, unsatisfied world, in the midst of its ambitious, jostling crowds, you had been blessed in knowing this man, contented to do his work, in his happy way, unheeding and unseeking the praise of man. Tenderly sacred to all who knew him is the memory of George Bradford.

CHAPTER VIII

THE CONCORD FARMER

He planted where the deluge plowed
His hired hands were wind and cloud
His eyes detect the Gods concealed
In the hummock of the field.

—Ralph Waldo Emerson

Husbandry is universally a sacred art—pursued with too much heedlessness and haste by us—To have large farms and large crops is our object. Our thoughts on this subject should be as slow and deliberate as the pace of the ox.

—Henry D. Thoreau, *Journal,* April 17, 1846

Above: Scene from *The New England Farmer*

ALTHOUGH EMERSON'S lectures in Boston on "Representative Men" had been a great success, he would later discover what he considered a serious omission. "Plainly," he wrote, "justice should have been done to the unexpressed greatness of the common farmer and laborer." The kind of person he had in mind was a far cry from the "gentleman farmer" of Brook Farm. Yet in Concord, at least, there was no sharp line drawn between the "intellectuals" and those who tilled their ancestral acres. Edmund Hosmer, convinced that the Brook Farm experiment was doomed to failure, nevertheless enjoyed his visits to this somewhat rarefied community, as he did his talks with Henry Thoreau on the shores of Walden Pond.

It is significant that the prestigious Social Circle included, in 1846, many farmers among its membership. For example, there was George Minot Barrett, a direct descendant of Concord's founder, the Reverend Peter Bulkeley. Barrett's father and grandfather had both taken part in the events of April 19, 1775; the former, age fourteen, had helped to conceal military stores from the British. Both had been teachers in the regional school. Another ancestor, an early graduate of Harvard, was remembered as an "excelling grammarian." Barrett himself was an extraordinarily capable and energetic farmer. As a boy he had become interested in sheep raising on the ancestral family farm of some 230 acres in the western part of Concord, near the Acton line. In summer he would pasture his flock, which at times numbered more than three hundred, in New Ipswich, New Hampshire. When sheep became less profitable, he had turned with equal devotion to stock raising.

In the words of his biographer, Barrett "was in the habit of saying that when he had once looked a cow in the face, with interest enough to make an offer for her, he could recognize that cow ever after as readily as he recognized a human acquaintance." (This with a herd of seventy-odd animals!) And he was equally devoted to his apple orchard on the slopes of Annursnack Hill, said to be the best such orchard in Concord, producing in good seasons more than a hundred barrels of cider. Barrett was "a solid, square, John Bull sort of man," recalled a friend, "the nearest parallel in this country, perhaps, of the best kind of English yeoman, or farmer, living on his own acres."

As Concord farmers enjoyed the company of the town's professionals—lawyers, doctors, clergymen, writers, editors—so city-bred youths, in their turn, felt that acquaintance with practical matters like farming was a necessary part of their education. George William Curtis (who would later become editor of *Harper's Weekly*) and his older brother James Burrill had been attracted to Concord by their intense admiration for Emerson, who believed that "the habit of living in the presence of these invitations of material wealth . . . has given a strong direction to the wishes and aims of active young men to withdraw from cities and cultivate the soil." The Curtis brothers boarded for three summers with different Concord farmers. "We first took up our residence," wrote Burrill, "in the family of an elderly farmer [Nathan Barrett] recommended by Mr. Emerson. We gave up half the day (except in hay-time, when we gave the whole day) to sharing the farm work indiscriminately with the farm laborers. The rest of the day we devoted to other pursuits. . . . (Crusty old Captain Barrett—possibly taken aback by those Raphaelesque ringlets—promptly set them to shoveling manure to "test their metal.") For our second season we removed to another farm and farmer's house near Mr. Emerson and Walden Pond . . . living in the very simplest and primitive style." Their landlord this time was Edmund Hosmer. "The people here who are worth knowing, I find live very quietly and retired," wrote George to their friend John S. Dwight of Brook Farm. "In the country friendship seems not to be of that consuming, absorbing character that city circumstances give it." And in words that bring to mind Thoreau's statement in *Walden* of his reasons for going to live alone in his cabin by the pond, George declared: "I want to drink this cup of farming to the bottom and taste not only the morning froth but the afternoon and evening strength of dregs and bitterness, if there be any." In fact, he and Henry were congenial from their first meeting. And by happy circumstance the Curtis brothers helped Henry prepare for his famous experiment in living. In early May of 1845 they had walked over to Walden Pond with Hosmer and his three sons to help Thoreau raise the frame of his cabin and put on the roof. No man, Henry later remarked, was more honored in the character of his raisers than he.

On their third return to Concord, the brothers boarded with Minot Pratt, on his farm near Punkatasset Hill. Pratt had begun life as a Boston printer and writer on agricultural subjects. Idealistic and high-minded, he and his wife had joined the Brook Farm community, worked hard to make it a success, and invested most of their capital in its future. When it eventually broke up and their stake in it was lost, they had settled down in Concord to make a living from the soil. Apparently they felt no bitterness about the cost to them of this ill-fated experiment. "For several years," wrote George Curtis, "Pratt was in the habit of gathering on the lawn in front of his house, under a large elm tree, a picnic of such of his

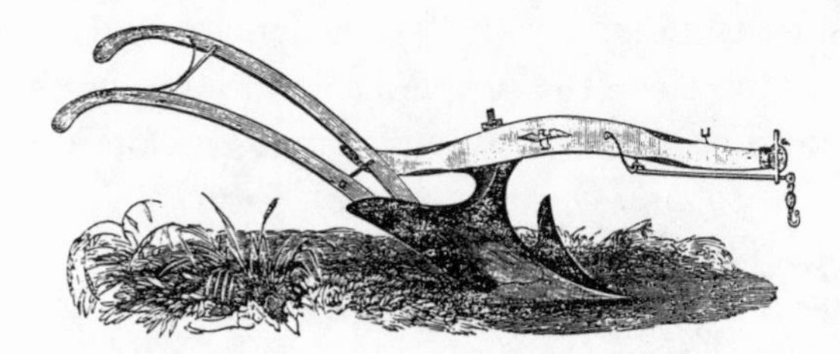

Brook Farm associates as he could bring together. Emerson, Phillips, Thoreau, Curtis, George Bradford, and others of note, often attended. The gathering was a delightful one, and it was made an occasion of happy reminiscences and a renewal of old personal ties and affections."

Not all was drudgery on Minot Pratt's farm. Louisa May Alcott recalled in later life the cornhusking parties the Pratts used to give for boys and girls in the neighborhood:

> "One beautiful evening under the September moon, Mr. and Mrs. Pratt summoned the Concord young people to their farm [on Punkatasset Hill] for a husking. We worked gayly at the piles of bleached gold leaves and stalks to get out the livelier gold within—the lanterns shining above, and the cows beside us creaking their stanchions. After an hour we passed across the moon-lit yard, under the most beautiful elm in Middlesex into the house where we washed our hands and brushed our clothes and were then invited into the kitchen to a supper by our hostess. There was a long table with a white cloth. In the centre, in a shining milk pan, was a mountain of white-blossomed popcorn, flanked by candles placed in sockets cut in the small ends of huge orange carrots. Next were baskets of apples, crimson and yellow and green, round towers of brown bread and fragrant soft gingerbread, with fresh cheese near by. There were candelabras made of inverted multiplex rutabagas, and here and there gleamed the tanned, yellow faces of pumpkin pies. The room was decorated with autumn leaves, probably scarlet and yellow maple, and blue gentians and asters.

Pratt's botanical training was of lasting value to his native town. He not only made a study of the flora of Concord but increased its variety by a particularly engaging hobby. In Louisa's words, "Whenever he could spare a day from the farm, he went afoot or in his wagon to some town where grew a flower which we had not, and set it out in some out-of-the-way spot in Concord wood or meadow. It is said that he increased our flora by some hundred varieties by this beneficence."

By no means the most prominent but perhaps the most endearing farmer in midcentury Concord was Emerson's close neighbor, George Minott—the town's "most poetical farmer," in Thoreau's estimation. Minott's small, square, one-storied, and unpainted house stood on Boston (Lexington) Road, partway up the south-facing slope of the hill opposite the Emersons. Minott was, recalled Waldo's son Edward,

> a descendant of one of the early Concord families, one who had never been in the railroad cars, nor but once to Boston . . . but one who knew Concord field and forest by heart—a man somewhat of the Rip van Winkle type. . . . He kept a cow and raised corn and "crooknecks" in his little field [which lay west of Emerson's study], eked out the larder of himself and his sister, the village tailoress, with duck and partridges, horn-pout and pickerel. He valued and took much leisure, and liked to gossip with Mr. Emerson over the fence about "the old bow-arrow times" when, as he averred, he had heard from the fathers, deer and otter and raccoons were common in Concord, and moose had been shot here.

Waldo himself took much delight in gossiping with his neighbor, "who busies himself all the year round under my windows, writes out his nature in a hundred works, in drawing water, hewing wood, building fence, feeding his cows, haymaking, and a few times in the year he goes into the woods. Thus his human spirit unites itself with nature."

Minot Pratt's "Boughy Elm." "At Pratt's, the stupendous, boughy, branching elm, like vast thunderbolts stereotyped on the sky; heaven-defying, sending back dark vegetable bolts, as if flowing back in the channel of the lightning."—Thoreau, *Journal.* (Photograph taken November 3, 1917)

Henry Thoreau particularly enjoyed hearing George Minott reminisce about the early days when, before the building of the milldam, he had caught a three-and-a-half-pound trout in Mill Brook; when he had seen mink running along the shore; and when he had watched a "partridge hawk" [peregrine falcon?] strike down a partridge and managed to secure it himself while the hawk kept out of gunshot. "I willingly listen," commented Thoreau, "to the stories he had told me half a dozen times already." And there was also another bond between the two men, one that Thoreau would discover some years after he had left Walden Pond. His bean field had once belonged "to Deacon George Minott, who lived in the house next below the East Quarter schoolhouse, and was a brother of my grandfather-in-law," Henry noted in his journal. And, one might add, who was directly descended from the Abbot of Walden in Essex, England.

Thoreau deplored the dreariness, the narrowness, and the financial pressures of many farmers' lives. But George Minott was a happy exception. "He does nothing with haste and drudgery, but as if he loved it," wrote Thoreau. "He makes the most of his labor, and takes infinite satisfaction in every part of it. He is not looking forward to the sale of his crops or any pecuniary profit, but he is paid by the constant satisfaction which his labor yields him. . . . He cares not so much to raise a large crop as to do his work well."

Thoreau's encomium is not surprising. Minott, in his way of life, embodied many of the principles by which Thoreau himself sought to live: simplicity, self-sufficiency, pride in craftsmanship, independence, and kinship with nature. Said Henry of his friend: "He loves to walk in a swamp in windy weather and hear the wind groan through the pines."

Although Emerson shared Thoreau's liking for George Minott, if he *had* included a farmer among his "representative men," there can be little doubt whom he would have chosen. He had already written an affectionate description of such an individual (more worldly than Minott), in an essay for the *Dial* entitled *Agriculture in Massachusetts:*

> In an afternoon in April, after a long walk, I traversed an orchard where two boys were grafting apple trees, and found the Farmer in his corn field. He was holding the plough, and his son driving the oxen. This man always impresses me with respect, he is so manly, so sweet-tempered, so faithful, so disdainful of all appearances, excellent and reverable in his old weather-worn cap and blue frock bedaubed with the soil of the field, so honest withal, that he always needs to be watched lest he should cheat himself. . . . As I drew near this brave laborer in the midst of his own acres, I could not help feeling for him the highest respect. . . . What good this man has, or has had, he has earned. No rich father or father-in-law left him with any inheritance of land or money. He borrowed the money with which he bought his farm, and has bred up a large family, given them a good education, and improved his land in every way year by year. . . . Toil has not broken his spirit. His laugh rings with the sweetness and hilarity of a child; yet he is a man of a strongly intellectual taste, of much reading, and of an erect good sense and independent spirit, which can neither brook usurpation nor falsehood in any shape.

Emerson did not identify this ideal farmer. But no one in Concord could fail to recognize Edmund Hosmer. A direct descendant of James Hosmer, one of the sixty-three original settlers of Concord in 1635, he was named after Edmund Burke, an intimate friend of the family in England. His father, a cabinetmaker and farmer, had fought in the Continental Army, beginning with the Battle of Concord and Lexington. The ninth of ten children, Edmund had been prevented by poor health from entering Harvard. Apparently he, like Emerson, had been threatened with consumption, of which many of his family members had died. After a sea voyage (the usual treatment at that time), he had purchased a farm on Lincoln Road in Concord, only a mile from the Emersons and even closer to Walden Pond.

In 1846 Hosmer was forty-eight years old—in Nathaniel Hawthorne's words, "a short and study personage of middle age, with a face of shrewd and kind expression and manners of natural courtesy." Hosmer "was in the habit of reading much and thinking more," recalled a friend who knew him at this time, and "was much of a philosopher and was very suggestive in his conversation." He had welcomed the Alcott family to his home after the demise of Fruitlands, when the eccentric Bronson was looked down upon by less open minded members of the community. And he understood Thoreau better than most. It was Henry's custom, while living at Walden, to dine on Sundays with the Emersons and to stop at the Hosmers' on his way back to the pond, often staying for supper. Edmund was, in Henry's opinion, "the most intelligent farmer in Concord, perchance in Middlesex."

On March 13, 1846, the *Concord Freeman* announced the schedule of events for the Middlesex Cattle Show and Ploughing Match, to take place in Concord on October 7: "The Society of Middlesex Husbandmen and Manufacturers hereby offer the following Premiums, for the encouragement of Agriculture, Manufacturing, and the cultivation of Trees, within the County of Middlesex." Under "Live Stock," prizes were offered for "the best Fat Ox, at least expense"; for the best bull and bull calf; for the best steer, milk cow, and yoke of working oxen; and for the best swine, both bear and breeding sow. Good forestry earned similar awards, with emphasis on the finest groves of white oak, white ash, elm, and sugar maple. Prizes for fruit orchards included apples (surely George Minott Barrett would have won some of these for his orchard on Annursnack Hill), peaches, and plums. There were contests for the best-cultivated farms and the greatest production per acre. From the spectators' point of view, the best part of the show must have been the Ploughing Match, "to owners of eight Ploughs, to be drawn by oxen," and the Trial of Working Oxen, which was to take place "immediately after the services in the Meeting House."

For onlookers as well as participants, the Cattle Show was the great event of the year. The farmers taking part in the 1846 show never doubted that, in recognizing the most skillful among them, they were celebrating a secure way of life. They would have agreed with Emerson that "every man has an exceptional respect for tillage, and the feeling that this is the original calling of his race. [The farmer] is permanent, clings to his land as the rocks do." But already the New England farmer's livelihood was threatened by competition from lands with fewer rocks. The Erie Canal had been in operation for some twenty years; wheat and other produce from the West were flooding the eastern markets. The sheep pastures of New England—cleared from the forest by incredible toil of men and oxen—and the rock farms with their thin skin of topsoil could not compete with the lush grasslands and rich black earth of the Midwest. Former pasture and cropland—as in Concord's Estabrook Country—was returning to woods. Great stone walls, forgotten cellar holes, would soon be the only mementos of a vanished era.

The Concord landscape in 1846 would have been barely recognizable to the original settlers. When they arrived from the well-kept farms of East Anglia, they were faced with heavily forested country; open space was confined largely to water meadows, bogs, and cornfields cleared by the Indians. Yet some two centuries later, only 11 percent remained wooded. Thoreau's cabin stood on one of the few large tracts of woodland left in town. In some areas, soil erosion, caused by overfarming, was already a problem. Tracts suitable only for forest had been cleared and farmed for a brief period and were now growing up to scrub*; local lumber was becoming scarce.

* The scrubland was not wholly worthless. For example, Thoreau's family had established its pencil factory to take advantage of the cedars that had colonized the abandoned fields.

Concord's best farmers, who had been tilling the same land for generations, had been good guardians of their inheritance. But now they were confronted with a new threat to their way of life: a development that would at once intensify the competition from the Midwest and make the Concord farmer increasingly dependent on the markets of Boston. Two years earlier, the Fitchburg Railroad, built largely by Irish immigrants, had reached Concord, its arrival celebrated by a gala opening on Bunker Hill Day in 1844. The journey to Boston that had taken four hours by coach could now be made in an hour. At Walden Pond, Henry Thoreau heard "the iron horse make the hills echo with his snort like thunder, shaking the earth with his feet, and breathing fire and smoke from his nostrils." He was well aware that the locomotive whistle was screaming a message from the city merchants that no farmer could ignore. "Nor is any man so independent on his farm that he can say them nay." The close link with Boston meant that the Concord farmer would henceforth be in competition with the outside world, no longer self-sufficient, no longer sure of the local market for his produce. Subsistence agriculture would slowly give way to an agriculture dependent on trade with the city.

There were compensations. Boston offered a ready market for dairy products and for perishable fruits and vegetables. Barely a year after the railroad reached town, Joseph D. Brown had established a successful dairy enterprise; a milk car was added to the morning train, and Concord's herds of dairy cattle began to grow. And in the winter of 1846 a new ice industry was established on Walden Pond. Hundreds of Irish workers came out daily by rail from Cambridge, sometimes harvesting as much as a thousand tons of ice a day. The ice was stored beside the tracks in huge piles up to thirty-five feet high, insulated with straw, to be shipped to Boston as needed.

The location of the railroad, which touched on the southwest corner of Walden Pond, had caused deep distress to citizens of Concord who valued the beauty and serenity of their countryside. While it was still being built, many of the town's most distinguished men and women, beginning with Emerson and Alcott, addressed a petition to the railroad's general manager:

> We citizens of Concord respectfully and urgently remind you that your contractors are now building the new line through what is to us and to all lovers of nature most precious ground. The No. Branch of Concord river is our "Central Park" and one of the most beautiful pieces of simple scenery in New England. We feel it is bad enough to have a railroad at all in that place, but the ruthless destruction of a single tree, or shrub, for fire wood or for any purpose not absolutely necessary to building the road will be viewed by us all as barbarism which we hope you can and will prevent.

(Although he had been the first to sign the petition warning the railroad managers against unnecessary destruction of the landscape, Emerson had been shrewd enough to buy several shares of stock, which quickly increased in value. More important to him—as he surely recognized—would be the extension of the territory in which he could deliver his lectures, on which he was largely dependent for his living.)

Henry Thoreau—who could hear "all of music" in the humming of a telegraph wire, discover Nova Zembla in a frozen swamp, and "go round the world by the Old Marlborough Road"—characteristically found unlikely virtues in the loaded freight cars heading west from Boston:

> I am refreshed and expanded when the freight-train rattles past me on the rail road—and I smell the stores which have been dispensing their odors from long-wharf last—which remind me of foreign parts of coral reefs & Indian oceans and tropical climes—& the extent of the globe—I feel more a citizen of the world at the sight of the palm leaf

> which will cover so many new England flaxen heads the next summer—the manilla cordage—& the cocoanut husks—The old Junk & scrap iron, and worn out sails—are full of history more legible & significant now these old sails than if they could be wrought into writing paper. Here goes lumber from the Maine woods which . . . so lately to wave over the bear & moose & caribou. This closed car smells of salt fish the strong scent—the commercial scent—reminding me of the grand banks & the fisheries & fish flakes.

Others in Concord were neither "refreshed" nor "expanded" but anxious and angry. The stagecoach and the freight team were doomed. "The teamsters," a townsman later recalled, "write on their teams, 'No monopoly, Old Union Line, Fitchburg, Groton, etc.' On the guide-boards they paint, 'Freetrade and Teamsters' rights.' " Nor were the tavern owners happy; with Boston now so close, there would be fewer stopovers by travelers from the West. And storekeepers on the Milldam would soon be competing for customers with shops in the big city. In short, the railroad, in operation to Concord for only two years, had not only begun to change the farmers' way of life; it had already demonstrated that this small, rural town could not long remain a metropolitan center for the region.

The warrant for the November 9, 1846, town meeting contained two significant items: "To know if the town will confirm the doings of the Selectmen in laying out certain town ways in the vicinity of the Railroad Depot" and "To hear the report of the Committee chosen to petition the County Commissioners for a further allowance from the County toward the cost of building the 'Factory Road.' " By now the arrival of the Fitchburg Railroad was already stimulating the growth of the area west of the center of Concord, known as Westvale or Factory Village, where the Assabet River provided a ready source of waterpower. Here stood the Loring Lead Works, manufacturers of lead pipe; the plant could now be reached by a spur of the railroad, of which David Loring was, conveniently, a director. Close by at Dodge's Pond was Dodge's Dyehouse. There were at least two sawmills in the area. And just over the line Nathan Pratt had his powder mill, a thriving establishment that, unfortunately, blew up from time to time.

Most important—and most enduring—was Damon's Mills, a mile and a half downstream from the powder mill. Its founder, Calvin Carver Damon, the son of a New Hampshire farmer, was born in 1803, the same year as Emerson. Though poorly educated, he was ambitious and enterprising, working his way up as a salesman, clerk, storekeeper, superintendent, and eventually owner of a woolen and cotton mill in Factory Village, where he developed a popular fabric known as dommet. (It is said that the Boston merchant who financed this enterprise was skeptical until he was shown the finished product. "Dom it!" he exclaimed, "*that* is *good cloth;* it will sell." And so it did.) By 1846 Calvin's son Edward Carver Damon, who would become famous in Concord history as the "Clothier of the Assabet," was ten years old. Four years later he wrote a letter to a cousin that gives a good idea of a mill hand's life in midcentury. (In this case, however, the mill hand was the owner's son.) "You want to know how I get along. I work in the cotton room tending drawing. It is very clean work for the factory. I go to work at seven and work half an hour, then half an hour for breakfast, then work again from eight o'clock to half-past twelve. Commence again at one o'clock and work until half-past seven. I like it very well." Quite a workday for a fourteen-year-old. But a bit better than that of the Lowell mill girls.

Factory Village had been developed largely by entrepreneurs from other areas, not by the established families of Concord. Unlike many other manufacturing districts in New England, it never grew so large and populous as to become a town in itself. As the annual Cattle Show gave witness, Concord in midcentury was a farmers' town.

CHAPTER IX

INSTRUCTION: SUNDAYS AND WEEKDAYS

If it were not for death and funerals, I think the institution of the church would not stand longer.

—Henry D. Thoreau, *Journal*

Above: The Unitarian Church

On March 24, 1846, Emerson wrote in his journal: "God builds his temple in the heart, on the ruins of churches and religions." More than thirteen years had passed since—after much soul-searching—he had resigned his ministry in Boston. After moving to Concord, however, he had continued to fill the pulpit on a part-time basis in neighboring towns, a practice that he found congenial, since it required no parish work. But eventually he had abandoned the pulpit altogether for the lecture platform and the lyceum, where he could speak his mind without restraint. In his Divinity School address at Harvard, he had really let himself go, as he excoriated the church and its ministers: "The priest's Sabbath has lost the splendor of nature; it is unlovely; we are glad when it is done. . . . We shrink as soon as the prayers begin, which do not uplift, but smite and offend us." Then came the passage that struck home—home to Concord: "I once heard a preacher who sorely tempted me to say, I would go to church no more. . . . A snow storm was falling around us. The snow storm was real; the preacher merely spectral; and the eye felt the sad contrast in looking at him, and then out of the window behind him, into the beautiful meteor of the snow." Emerson was quoting from his journal. The "preacher" was the minister of the First Parish Church in Concord, the Reverend Barzillai Frost.

Frost had come to Concord straight from Harvard Divinity School. Born on a small New Hampshire farm and having lost his father while still an infant, he had a deprived and sober childhood. Hard work and a devotion to "self-improvement" had seen him through Phillips Exeter Academy and Harvard College. He was a good man but a limited one. He thought by the book and he preached by the book, maintaining, for example, that the miracles described in the New Testament established the divinity of Christ, and that was that. Yet oddly enough, Frost may have played a decisive role in shaping Emerson's career. Apparently Waldo, listening to Barzillai's soporific sermons, came to think of him as representing the church as a whole and everything that was wrong with it.

The late Dana McLean Greeley, writing about his predecessors in the First Parish, speculates on how Emerson might have felt about the church (and how those views might have affected his career) had a more liberal, more dynamic minister been chosen to succeed the venerable Ezra Ripley. For instance, suppose that the church committee had selected Emerson's close friend Theodore Parker, who, like him, was "a prophet of the new Unitarianism or natural religion, embodying the affirmation of the total humanity of Jesus and the universality of the religious experience," a freethinker, and one of the most inspiring preachers of his time. This notion is not idle speculation; Parker had applied for the job at the same time as Frost but had been rejected. Had Parker been chosen, would Emerson have attacked the clergy as violently as he did in the Divinity School address? Would he have broken so completely with the church?

In 1846 all this was past history. Barzillai Frost had been Concord's minister for eight years; Waldo and he were on friendly terms. But on Sundays Waldo was inclined to stay home. As for other members of the family, it was up to them. "He was glad to have us go to church," his son recalled. "It was only a question for each person where the best church was,—in the solitary wood, the chamber, the talk with the serious friend, or in hearing the preacher." Most of Concord's parishioners were well satisfied with their minister. "Let no man undervalue Barzillai Frost," wrote George Frisbie Hoar. "He was a great power and influence in the town for righteousness and good learning."

The First Parish Church was no longer the only church in Concord. Two decades earlier, a small group of the more conservative parishioners, discontented with the direction the First Parish was taking, had broken away to form the Second Congregational Society, which had a Calvinistic minister to teach "piety, religion, and morals." They had built a new meetinghouse on Walden Street, and their numbers had grown rapidly. But there was little sense of rivalry, and the two churches kept on cordial terms with each other.

Less important in terms of numbers, but with a character of its own, was the Universalist Society: a small group presided over by an energetic and outspoken young minister named Addison Grant Fay, who had married a Concord woman and was raising a family in a small cottage on Monument Street. "His preaching," recalled a friend, "was direct, pungent, and, I suspect, a little careless as to whom or what it hit, so long as he believed that the whom or what deserved to be hit." Fay had a dry sense of humor. When two neighbors who were financial supporters of his parish—but deeply involved in the liquor business—remonstrated with him for preaching on the subject of temperance, he replied: "Gentlemen, I do not know that I am above the weakness of other people; and if my salary were fifteen hundred or two thousand dollars, considering your position, perhaps I should be tempted to hold my tongue. But on four hundred and fifty dollars I think I can afford to keep a conscience."

By 1846 Fay had decided that he could not support a family on that salary and had convinced himself that he was "cut out for business." So during the course of the year he resigned and Concord lost its most colorful preacher. (Eventually Fay became manager of the powder mill at Assabet Village and lost his life in an explosion.)

District School, Barrett's Mill Road

What does education do? It makes a straight-cut ditch of a free, meandering brook.

—Henry D. Thoreau, *Journal*

Since childhood, the desire for education had been a driving force in Barzillai Frost's life. He had been the top scholar at Exeter (in the class that included Charles Sumner); he had paid his way through Harvard by schoolteaching in Framingham; and, while attending Divinity School, he had taught mathematics and "natural philosophy" (i.e., science) to college undergraduates. Thus it is not surprising that he had been put on the Concord School Committee immediately on being hired for the church. The two institutions were close; no one was as yet concerned about separation of church and state in the public schools.

On April 6, 1846, the Concord town meeting voted to spend two thousand dollars "for support of schools"—by far the largest appropriation of town funds. The report of the school committee, prepared by the chairman, Barzillai Frost, was read and accepted. School regulations adopted early in the century included the teaching of "virtue, morality and piety." Education of children at public expense was by now firmly established, though it had not come about without a struggle. As recently as 1840, only half of New England's children had been given free schooling. Certain class-conscious conservatives had argued against providing education to those who were "better suited to their station without it." Others contended that industrial prosperity depended on an abundant supply of labor "comparatively uneducated" (an opinion clearly not shared by the mill owners of Lowell). Neither of these bizarre ideas was relevant to Concord, which was neither an industrial nor a class-conscious community.

In 1846 the town maintained no fewer than ten schools in seven districts, with a total of 525 pupils, ranging in age from four to sixteen. These were still the days of the "little red schoolhouse," one teacher to each school. Along with the three R's, the children studied traditional subjects such as spelling and geography. The school committee noted the need for globes and maps and acknowledged the generous gift from Mr. Alcott of two maps to the No. 2 district school on Lexington Road—doubtless the one his daughters attended. At the center of town stood the brick "grammar school," the preparatory school for college, which offered instruction in Greek and Latin. The teachers there were men, but both men and women taught in the primary schools.

Discipline was strict. For older boys, this meant frequent use of the ferule. But—as Judge Hoar recalled—in the "infant

The Nine Acre Corner District School

schools" that were kept by women, discipline was not so severe:

> The schoolmistress in those days wore what was called a busk—a flat piece of lancewood, hornbeam, or some other like tough and elastic wood, thrust into a sort of pocket or sheath in her dress, which came up almost to the chin and came down below the waist. This was intended to preserve the straightness and grace of her figure. When the small boy misbehaved, the schoolma'am would unsheath this weapon, and for some time thereafter the culprit found sitting down exceedingly uncomfortable. Sometimes the sole of the schoolmistress's slipper answered the same purpose, and sometimes a stick from some neighboring birch-tree. It all came to pretty much the same thing in the end.

Many of the teachers, of course, came from local families; few had any special qualifications. Though the Concord School Committee felt strongly that the "moral principles and social refinement" of the town depended on the quality of its schools, the fact is that teaching was only beginning to be regarded as a serious profession.

The committee, however, took its job seriously. The schools were visited by at least one member no fewer than 141 times in the course of the year. (1846 was the first year in which the committee's report was published.) School committee members encouraged the pupils to think for themselves rather than just learning by rote; during the past year they had noted great improvement in the students' use of the blackboard "in explaining processes and giving reasons." They chose the material for examinations, which were open to parents and the public and which apparently stressed reading out loud; in 1846 the committee members were particularly gratified that an earlier "artificial and monotinous [*sic*] cadence and unnatural tones of voice" had been replaced by a more natural style, closer to the student's own and indicating some understanding of what was being read. Particularly appropriate, considering the political tensions of the time, was the committee's recommendation that "every young man" (not "young woman") learn the principles of his government and of his national and state constitutions; in a democracy "where every man is a legislator" it was dangerous, then as now, to be ignorant of how the government worked.

The school year had both winter and summer terms. As in any farming community, attendance was governed in part by the weather and the state of the crops. "Keep your boys and girls in school as long as you can spare them from spring work," advised the *Concord Freeman* on March 6, "but never lament that you cannot spare them in summer." Truancy was high throughout the year—and no wonder, considering the stifling atmosphere of the schoolrooms, overheated by smoky wood stoves, poorly ventilated, and odorous—so close that, during a school committee visit, one member had to leave the room after thirty minutes. "The first and most sacred duty of every teacher" stated the committee's report, "is to attend to the temperature and ventilation of the school room." By now many of the old buildings were in bad shape, too rickety to be worth repairing. There was to be "no more patching up of old school houses," stated the committee firmly. Already a fine new school was under construction on Lowell Road: a "tasteful little temple of learning," with classic proportions and a playground graced by trees and shrubs.

All in all, 1846 was a good school year—though somewhat marred by difficulties that had sprung up between two schoolmasters and some of the "larger scholars." Following an investigation by the committee, one of the teachers was dismissed, owing to "facts of a moral nature which the investigation elicited."

For boys seeking a college education—in most cases, preparing for admission to Harvard—there was the center school, with its emphasis on the classics; and there was Concord Academy, a private school where the Thoreau brothers had taught before John's untimely death. There were also opportunities for private tutoring; George Bradford, for example, after leaving Brook Farm, had served as tutor to the Emerson children in Concord. Ties with Harvard had always been close, both in Concord and in neighboring Lincoln, where, in the late eighteenth century, the Reverend Charles Stearns had found time from his parish duties to prepare no less than forty boys for admission to the college—including Samuel Hoar and Nathan Brooks, both of whom would become successful Concord lawyers. (Stearns' school had also admitted young women—one of the first in America to do so.) Emerson and Thoreau were, of course, Harvard graduates, though Henry would later disparage the importance of his college training. Once when Emerson spoke of being on the lookout for great poets and orators, Thoreau remarked that he had found one, in the woods, "but it had feathers and had not been to Harvard College."

Harvard had been the scene of two major events in Emerson's career: his Phi Beta Kappa oration, "The American Scholar" (in 1837), which first brought him wide public attention, and a year later the Divinity School address, which delighted liberal thinkers but infuriated the clergy at large and specifically Harvard's professor of sacred literature, Andrews Norton, who replied with "A Discourse on the Latest Form of Infidelity."

By 1846 Emerson's reputation for scholarship was well established, and the thunderous attacks on his religious views were but a distant rumble. On April 30 he took the "cars" to Cambridge to attend the inauguration of a new president of the college, Edward Everett. Emerson was already acquainted with Everett, formerly a professor of Greek literature, a congressman, and—when Emerson had delivered his Phi Beta Kappa oration—governor of Massachusetts. On that last occasion Everett had warmly congratulated him on his speech and had recalled with affection Waldo's brothers, the late Edward and Charles, both of whom had been high honor students.

The inauguration ceremonies were impressive and prolonged. The *Concord Freeman* reported on the activities of this no-doubt-exhausting day. Governor Briggs delivered to the incoming president the original charter of the university—a "venerable old parchment." Everett spoke for an hour and a quarter. There was a dinner for five hundred in Harvard Hall; "Dr. O. W. Holmes convulsed the audience with laughter with a humorous political production." Later there were fireworks. Daniel Webster spoke both at church and at dinner. The following morning, Emerson wrote in his journal: "I was at Cambridge yesterday to see Everett inaugurated. His political brothers came as if to bring him to the convent door, and to grace with a sort of bitter courtesy his taking of the cowl. . . . Webster I could so willingly have spared on this occasion." Emerson considered Webster to be Everett's "evil genius," the person who had diverted him from his true calling as a scholar to the world of politics. "Well," Emerson wrote, "this Webster must needs come into the house just at the moment when Everett was rising to make his Inaugural Speech. Of course, the whole genial current of feeling flowing toward him was arrested, and the old Titanic Earth-Son was alone seen." Emerson complained in his journal that these college events were no longer literary but political; a man of letters would feel out of place. And much as he admired Everett, he found the close of his inaugural speech "chilling and melancholy. With a coolness indicating absolute scepticism and despair, he deliberately gave himself over to the corpse-cold Unitarianism and Immortality of Brattle Street and Boston."

Although, as a man of letters, Emerson may have felt out of place at Harvard, the college library was indispensable to him, as the following letter, dated June 25, 1846, makes clear. (In view of the contrast with today's computerized library practice, it seems worth quoting in full.)

To the Corporation of Harvard University.

Gentlemen,

I request the privilege of borrowing books from the College Library, subject to usual rules for their safety & return. I do not find myself included in any class of persons entitled by law to this privilege. I ask it as an alumnus of the College engaged in literary pursuits, & constantly in want of books which only the University can supply, & which it has provided for precisely such needs as mine; and as, in my residence, conveniently situated for easy access to Cambridge.

> I have formally endeavored to borrow books by special orders signed, in each case, by the President. But this mode is very troublesome to the President, & very inconvenient to the borrower. It may easily happen, as it has happened to me, that after I have selected my books at the Library, the President is not at home, or not at liberty; then I must return to my house, fourteen miles distant, without them.
>
> Presuming the willingness of the Corporation to extend the usefulness of their valuable Library to the utmost limits compatible with safety, I pray them to grant me the right of taking books thence, from time to time, in my own name.
>
> R. Waldo Emerson

He sent a copy of the letter to Harvard's new president, who promptly saw to it that the University's distinguished alumnus got his wish.

In late August, Emerson was again in Cambridge, this time for a happier occasion: Harvard Commencement and the twenty-fifth reunion of his class of 1821. There were nineteen present, and, Emerson noted, "a very cordial three hours' space we spent together." He had been asked to speak for the group, which he did with warmth and with commendable brevity—in contrast to the commencement exercises, which, the *Freeman* reported, included twenty-seven speakers and a fifteen-minute Latin oration that "riveted the attention of the audience." Twenty-year-old George Frisbie Hoar, son of Concord's Squire Hoar, glorified Daniel Boone as "the last representative of the heroic age of this country." Other speakers attacked "popery" and, in the spirit of the Mexican War, declared the Spanish character to be "unfit for the business of peopling a new country." On the following day the Harvard chapter of Phi Beta Kappa held its annual Literary Exercises, an event that Emerson doubtless found more congenial. The oration was delivered by Charles Sumner, abolitionist (and future senator); the poem, by Waldo's good friend and member of the Transcendental Club, the Reverend James Freeman Clarke. And the occasion must have brought to Emerson happy recollections of his own Phi Beta Kappa oration nine years earlier, a milestone on the road he had chosen for himself.

> *The one hundred and twenty-five dollars which is subscribed in this town every winter for a Lyceum is better spent than any other equal sum. Instead of noblemen, let us have noble towns or villages of men.*
>
> —Henry D. Thoreau, *Journal*

Long before the phrase *adult education* came into common usage, the concept behind it—the urge for self-improvement—had been generally accepted by all classes of society in New England. In 1826 a Millbury, Massachusetts, farmer named Josiah Holbrook, inspired by Yale's great teacher of natural science, Benjamin Silliman, had launched the lyceum movement. It was already flourishing three years later when the Concord Lyceum was founded. With the Honorable John Keyes as chairman, Mr. Lemuel Shattuck (who would later write a history of the town) as secretary, and fifty-seven members, the group began meeting Wednesday evenings at "the centre brick school house." At every second meeting there was a lecture, and each member was allowed to bring two ladies. By 1846 meetings were being held in the vestry of the Unitarian Church.

Normally the subjects were uncontroversial and somewhat academic, reflecting the thirst for knowledge characteristic of the time, in all walks of life. Early in 1846, members and their guests had listened to lectures on "ancient Egypt," on "The Colonial History of Massachusetts," and on technical subjects like mining and hydraulics and physiology. They heard Charles Sumner discuss "The Value of Time" and Henry Thoreau speak about Thomas Carlyle.

On March 24 Emerson delivered the first of six lectures on "Representative Men"—the same that he had given in Boston.* When he took the podium, his audience must have been prepared for substantial intellectual fare. But as the record shows, not all his "representative men" were familiar names to his hearers—least of all to the lyceum's secretary, Cyrus Stow, who had just taken over that office and whose minutes recorded lectures by R. Waldo Emerson on "Sweadingburg," "Montane," "Gothe," and "Napoleun Boneapart." Not everyone in the audience knew what Emerson was talking about. In *Remembrances of Emerson,* John Albee recalled that "it became the fashion to listen to Emerson's lectures and to ask what they meant; or to refer to some one who professed to understand them. The enchantment of his voice and presence moved nearly all auditors to a state of exaltation like fine music, and like the effects of music his was a mood hard to retain. It needed a frequent repetition, and those who heard him oftenest, at length became imbued with the spirit of his teachings and could appropriate as much as belonged to them; and some who doubtless carried away but little were self-pleased and thought they saw a new light. A small farmer of Concord told me proudly that he had heard every one of Emerson's lectures delivered in that town. After a moment's hesitation he added, 'And I understood 'em, too.' "

Emerson's close friend Sarah Ripley, probably the best-educated woman in Concord, admitted that she could not always follow her friend's flights into the empyrean. "Tomorrow Mr. Emerson . . . has promised to bring a lecture 'which has legs,' but I fear, after all, wings will be sprouting out at the heels."

*This was contrary to Emerson's usual practice of trying out his lectures on the Concord audience (to whom they were delivered free of charge) before taking them elsewhere.

On at least one occasion, a literary reference in the lyceum series was misinterpreted. In his lecture on Plato, Emerson said that the Greek philosopher "turned everything to the use of his philosophy, that 'wife, children and friends were all ground into paint' "—alluding to Washington Allston's story of the Paint King who married a lovely maiden that he might make paint of the beautiful color of her cheeks. "A worthy farmer's wife in the audience," recalled George F. Hoar, "took this literally, and left the room in high dudgeon. She said she thought Waldo Emerson might be in better business than holding up to the people of Concord the example of a wicked man who ground his wife and children into paint."

Much of the impact of Emerson's lectures was in the delivery. Reading his words today, one tries in vain to imagine what it would have been like to be in the room with him. Bronson Alcott recorded his own impression of the almost-hypnotic effect Emerson apparently had as a speaker: "We admire the stately sense, the splendor of diction. . . . Even his hesitancy between delivery of his periods, his perilous passages from paragraph to paragraph of manuscript, we have almost learned to like, as if he were but sorting his keys meanwhile for opening his cabinets . . . and we wait willingly till his gem is out glittering; admire the setting, too, scarcely less than the jewel itself." Alcott went on to make a comment that his friend might have found startling: "The order of ideas, of imagination, is observed in the arrangement, not that of logical sequence. You may begin at the last paragraph and read backwards."

Emerson's literary contemporaries were duly impressed. To Oliver Wendell Holmes, "He seemed like an exotic transplanted from some angelic nursery." "Emerson," wrote Holmes to Edward Everett Hale, "is the Buddha of the West." Herman Melville remarked sardonically, "Had [Emerson] lived in those days when the world was made, he might have offered some valuable suggestions." But Melville was also impressed: "Yet I think Emerson is more than a brilliant fellow. Be his stuff begged, borrowed, or stolen, or of his own domestic manufacture, he is an uncommon man. Swear he is a humbug—then he is no common humbug."

In some respects, young people may have understood Emerson better than did their parents. An old farmer, when asked it he understood Emerson, replied, "No, but my daughters swear by him." In any case, the Concord Lyceum lectures were social events as well as educational experiences. As one young man remarked, "I have attended all but one, and have taken a lady every time." Nevertheless, as Edward Emerson pointed out, "Improvement, not amusement, was the expectation."

CHAPTER X

THE LITERARY SCENE

The best you can write will be the best you are.
—Henry D. Thoreau, *Journal*

Above: Nathaniel Hawthorne. From an oil painting by Charles Osgood (Courtesy of the Essex Institute, Salem, Massachusetts)

EMERSON DELIVERED his final lecture, "Uses of Great Men," on April 29, 1846. The Concord Lyceum would have no more speakers until late in the year. Meanwhile, Concord residents enjoyed a literary event that came close to home, though the man responsible was no longer in town. In early June, Wiley and Putnam of New York published Nathaniel Hawthorne's *Mosses from an Old Manse.*

Thanks to Emerson and Elizabeth Hoar, Nathaniel and his bride, Sophia Peabody, had come straight from their wedding, in the summer of 1842, to the old parsonage beside the Battle Ground. It had been built by Waldo's grandfather, lived in for sixty years by the Reverend Ezra Ripley, and, since Ezra's death, owned by his son Samuel, a minister in Waltham. For Nathaniel and Sophia, the secluded dwelling beside the Concord River had been a sort of paradise on earth. "We seem to have been translated to the other state of being, without having passed through death," he noted a month after their arrival. Alas, paradise was short-lived. In the fall of 1845, after they had spent three idyllic years, their landlord retired from his ministry in Waltham and returned with his wife, Sarah, to the house where he was born. Reluctantly, the Hawthornes moved to Nathaniel's native Salem, where, in the spring of 1846, he obtained a job as surveyor of the Custom House.

By now, many Concord readers were familiar with Hawthorne's work. A year younger than Emerson, he had already begun writing for publication when he was in his twenties. Recently *Grandfather's Chair,* a new edition of *Twice-Told*

Tales, and *The Celestial Railroad* had kept his name before the public. Emerson had read him but without enthusiasm. "N. Hawthorne's reputation as a writer," he confided to his journal, "is a very pleasing fact, because his writing is not good for anything, and this is a tribute to the man." Fiction was not high on Waldo's reading list. But he had found this shy, retiring man to be an ideal walking companion. Nathaniel, wrote Sophia Hawthorne, "seems to fascinate Mr. Emerson. Whenever he comes to see him, he always takes him away so that no one may interrupt him in close and dead-set attack upon his ear. . . . E.[lizabeth] Hoar says that persons about Mr. E. so generally echo him, that it is refreshing to him to find this perfect individual all himself and nobody else." Like Emerson, Hawthorne had arrived in Concord determined to do nothing against his own genius. Here he found the freedom and privacy he had sought. To the inhabitants of Concord, however, he was, in George Curtis's words, "as much a phantom and a fable as the old pastor of the parish, dead half a century before." In Emerson's study, Curtis recalled, it seemed always morning; in the Hawthorne's parlor it was forever afternoon.

To Hawthorne, the characters attracted to the village by Emerson's presence appeared to be an odd lot. "Severe and sober as was the Old Manse," he wrote in the opening chapter of *Mosses,* "it was necessary to go but a little way beyond its threshold before meeting with stranger moral shapes of men than might have been encountered elsewhere in a circuit of a thousand miles. These hobgloblins of flesh and blood were attracted thither by the widespreading influence of a great original thinker, who had his abode at the opposite extremity of our village." Hawthorne himself felt no need for Emerson's philosophy. But he enjoyed their meetings at the Manse and their walks through the woods. "It was impossible to dwell in his [Emerson's] vicinity without inhaling more or less the mountain atmosphere of his lofty thought . . . and he is so quiet, so simple, so without pretention, encountering each man alive as if expecting to receive more than he could impart."

When *Mosses* was published some eight months after the Hawthornes left Concord, men and women who had been Nathaniel's neighbors for three years came to know him better by his writing than they had ever been able to do in person. (An anonymous letter to the *Concord Freeman* recommended the book on the grounds that it would give some hint to "his neighbors and townsmen, whose Yankee curiosity may have been excited by the mystery and seclusion in which he seemed to wrap himself when among us, in what manner some at least of his quiet hours were employed.") Publication was in two editions: a set of two paperbound volumes for a dollar, and a one-volume, cloth-bound edition for a dollar and a quarter. The author himself was not wholly satisfied with what he had written; he felt that he might have produced something more substantial than another volume of short stories. But to Concord readers the opening chapter, "The Old Manse," must have been particularly endearing, evoking as it did the spirit of the village in days gone by. Hawthorne had a yearning for the dark, mysterious past. He had made the most of the manse's age and seclusion: its small, old-fashioned windowpanes; its dusty attic filled with long-forgotten sermons; its walls "blackened with the smoke of unnumbered years, and made still blacker by the grim prints of Puritan ministers that hung around." Hawthorne found inspiration in the dark, brooding, nightmare forest of the early Puritans, the heathen wilderness that surrounds every village and every human soul. Here the witches held their Sabbath, here young Goodman Brown kept his tryst with the

Devil, amid "the creaking of the trees, and howling of wild beasts, the yell of Indians . . . as if all Nature were laughing him to scorn."

Publication of *Mosses from an Old Manse* was an important event for Concord. And the author, despite his reservations, must have been pleased with the professional notices. Reviewers praised it as "honestly American"—at a time when American literature was still in the process of establishing its independence from Europe's. "Hawthorne is national—" a critic wrote, "national in subject, in treatment and in manner." Others remarked on his graceful humor, his lack of self-consciousness and self-display—in contrast to many other American writers. Emerson, no enthusiast for Hawthorne's writing, observed in his journal: "Hawthorne invites his readers too much into his study, opens the process before them. As if the confectioner should say to his customers, 'Now, let us make the cake.' "

Some two months after publication, the author's friend Henry Thoreau went for a brief walking trip in the White Mountains of New Hampshire. As he sat beside the ruins of an old mill on the Pemigewasset River "where now the ivy grew and the trout glanced through the raceway and the flume," Henry's thoughts turned back to Concord and the Old Manse, to the legendary Ezra Ripley, and to the "youthful pastor" who had always been a welcome guest at the hut on Walden Pond. He wrote in his journal:

> But now no war nor battle's sound
> Invades this peaceful battle ground
> But waves of Concord murmuring by
> With sweetly fluent harmony.
> But since we sailed, some things have failed
> And many a dream gone down the stream
> Here then a venerable shepherd dwellt
> Who to his flock his substance dealt

And ruled them with a vigorous crook
By precept of the sacred Book.
But he the pierless bridge passed o'er
And now the solitary shore
Knoweth his trembling steps no more.
Anon a youthful pastor came
Whose crook was not unknown to fame
His lambs he viewed with gentle glance
Dispersed o'er a wide expanse,
And fed with "mosses from the Manse"
We view the rocky shore where late
With soothed and patient ear we sat
Under our Hawthorne in the dale
And listen to his Twice told Tale.

Thoreau himself had been busy at Walden Pond finishing the manuscript of *A Week on the Concord and Merrimack Rivers*. From time to time he had read earlier drafts to his friends to get their opinions. Hawthorne had written to his own publishers, Wiley and Putnam, who were on the lookout for promising American authors to counter the flood of books from England that had dominated the market. In reply to an inquiry from the firm's editor, he had suggested Thoreau as a possible prospect—but with due warning:

> As for Thoreau, there is one chance in a thousand that he might write a most excellent and readable book; but I should be sorry to take the responsibility, either towards you or him, of stirring him up to write anything. . . . He is the most unmalleable fellow alive—the most tedious, tiresome, and intolerable—the narrowest and most notional—and yet, true as all this is, he has great qualities of intellect and character. The only way, however, in which he could ever approach the popular mind, would be by writing a book of simple observation of nature, somewhat in the vein of White's *History of Selbourne*.

In fact, Thoreau was already engaged on such a book: one that would contain far more than "simple observation of nature" and that would make him famous. But now his immediate concern was to finish *The Week*. By mid-March the job was done. One afternoon he read the manuscript to Emerson as they sat beneath an oak tree on the bank of the Concord River. Waldo was delighted with it and wrote to Wiley and Putnam recommending it for their "American Library," in a letter more likely to appeal to a commercial publisher than Hawthorne's had been: "This book has many merits. It will be as attractive to *lovers of nature,* in every sense, that is, to naturalists, and to poets, as Isaak Walton. It will be attractive to scholars for its excellent literature, & to all thoughtful persons for its originality & profoundness. The narrative of the little voyage, though faithful, is a very slender thread for such big beads & ingots as are strung on it. It is really a book of the results of studies of years."

The firm agreed to publish but to do so only at the author's expense. This Henry could not afford. Accordingly, the manuscript was returned, despite Emerson's recommendation. (It would not be published for another three years—benefiting, however, from the further work that Thoreau put into it.)

Henry Thoreau was not the only writer whom Emerson was willing to sponsor. Early in the year Waldo had been unexpectedly faced with an urgent demand on both his time and his pocketbook. His young protégé and nearby neighbor, William Ellery Channing (nephew and namesake of the great Unitarian minister), had decided that, to be a true poet, one had to know Europe. Ellery, said Nathaniel Hawthorne, was "one of those queer and clever young men whom Mr. Emerson (that everlasting rejecter of all that is, and seeker for he knows not what) is continually picking up by way of a genius." Ellery was a character: sensitive, idealistic, deeply appreciative of natural beauty, one of the few companions that Henry Thoreau would tolerate on his normally solitary rambles—a personality, thought Henry, "as naturally whimsical as a cow is brindled." Also, perhaps, a bit spoiled. He *had* to go abroad—and right away. Who would pay for his passage?

With characteristic generosity, Emerson undertook to help. He wrote to a well-to-do friend, Samuel Gray Ward: "Ellery Channing has suddenly found out that he must see Europe, that he must see it now—nay, that it is a matter of life and death that he should set out for Havre and Italy on the first of March. . . . He thinks it indispensable that he should see buildings, and pictures, and mountains, and peasantries, part of his poetic education—never was a poet who did not see them." Emerson asked for—and probably got—fifty dollars from Ward. He himself chipped in seventy-five. Channing set sail in early March.

The presence of the Channing family in Concord and their close ties with the Emersons were in large part the work of Ellery's sister-in-law, the learned, formidable, persistent, and adoring friend of Waldo, Margaret Fuller. Margaret was not too happy when, five years earlier, her pretty, demure younger sister Ellen married Channing. From the start Margaret had felt protective about the young couple. Once, at the "earnest request" of Ellery, she had asked whether the Channings might live as boarders in the Old Manse. Hawthorne was horrified. He replied, as politely as he could, that "the comfort of both parties would be put in great jeopardy."

Margaret's initial reservations about her sister's marriage had been justified more than once. "The more responsibility was placed upon Ellery," she complained, "the more he would flee from it." Two years earlier, when their first child was born, Ellery had found the experience too much of a strain on his nerves and had gone off on a walking trip in the Catskills with Thoreau. This time, when the second child was about to arrive (the baby we met earlier having its cold bath), he felt an urgent need to take ship for Europe.

Emerson's main objective during the spring and summer was to prepare his own volume of poems for the press. He had hoped to accomplish this task shortly after the conclusion of the lecture series in Boston, but there seemed to be countless demands on his time. He had, for example, undertaken early in the year to arrange for the American publication, on reasonable terms, of the works of his great friend Thomas Carlyle—a far more time-consuming business than his sponsorship of Thoreau and Channing. At a time when there was no effective international copyright and American publishers competed ruthlessly for first chance at a popular English author, Carlyle's affairs were in a mess. Thanks to Emerson, he managed to get a fair deal at a time when he needed every cent he could earn. On April 18, 1846, Carlyle wrote Emerson to express his gratitude: "You have made the best of bargains for me, once again, with the freest contempt of trouble on your part, which I cannot sufficiently wonder at."

Waldo could be practical and patient in helping others. As for himself, he said (in a letter to Elizabeth Hoar in July), "The hankering remains to write and write—absolutely without reference to subject matter; and I respect a fact so unaccountable. We should be no better than parsnips, if we could not still look over our shoulders at the Power that drives us, and escape from private insignificance into a faith in the transcendant significance of our doing and being. . . . However, I wrote lately some verses . . . which I shall be impatient to show you."

Though Waldo had always wanted to be a poet, he was aware of the hurdles he faced. "The muse demands real sacrifices," he had recently commented in his journal. "You cannot be a poet and a paterfamilias and a militia captain." Yet for some time he had been showing his poetry to his friends, and many of his poems had appeared in magazines. Now at last he felt ready to collect them in a book. The young, lively Caroline Sturgis, a friend of the Emersons who earlier had been introduced to the Concord circle by Margaret Fuller, had been urging him to publish. She told him frankly, however, that she found his poetry too abstract; for her there was too little emotion, too much philosophy. Margaret had expressed much the same opinion: "His powers are mostly philosophical. . . . They want the simple force of nature and passion." Yet both she and Caroline found much meaning and beauty in certain passages.

By September the collection was in the hands of the printers. Wiley and Putnam had offered to publish it in their Library of American Books, in the same inexpensive format as their edition of Edgar Allan Poe's latest book, *The Raven and Other Poems*. But Waldo wanted something more attractive. He made an arrangement with James Munroe and Company of Boston, which had published his essays. On Christmas Day a handsome volume in white covers, entitled simply *Poems*, came on the market.

Reactions were mixed. The reviewer for the *Boston Courier* found it "one of the most peculiar and original volumes of poetry ever published in the United States": refined and subtle but also obscure. As for obscurity, Waldo seems almost to have been challenging his critics by leading off with an odd poem entitled "The Sphinx." Printed earlier in the *Dial*, it had been found puzzling by its readers. Even Henry Thoreau was baffled; he tried hard, but he was afraid that his attempt at explanation would be "as enigmatical as the Sphinx's riddle." Not so Henry Wadsworth Longfellow, to whom Emerson had sent an early copy of *Poems*. His good friend, never at a loss for words, went overboard. Two days after publication, he wrote Waldo from Cambridge that his wife had read the poems to him out loud. "A precious volume! The very Gold-coast of Song; along which we sailed, enjoying delicious sights and sounds of Nature and seeing the auriferous streams pour out their tribute into the sea. . . . A signal triumph awaits you, or rather attends you; and, believe me, among all your admirers none will more heartily rejoice in your success than I shall. The only bad thing about it is, that I shall never get my wife to read any more of my poems, you have fascinated her so with yours!"

In the same letter, Longfellow acknowledged receipt of a new volume of Ellery Channing's poems, which, he wrote, "does not command the spontaneous admiration which I like so much to feel." (Channing had—surprisingly—returned from abroad in early summer, apparently having decided that it was not, after all, a matter of life and death for him to get a European education.)

Waldo's Aunt Mary Moody Emerson was less than enthusiastic about either volume. Channing's verse she found offensive: "I'm weary, and nothing to read but this *Festus,* which I can't afford to read in good hours, and it adds to poor ones by its scavenger and its voluptuous expressions of love." Of Emerson's own poems she wrote with resignation: "Poems of the present day, to the grannies, is like setting meat and luxuries before the dead—for we hasten where the Sphinxes are not putting forth hands and feet for fours, but problems of high destiny which ages only may solve."

Among his Concord friends, Emerson could always count on Bronson Alcott to admire his poems with reserve. In his journal for June 28, Bronson commented on an afternoon that they spent together: "Now he is busy preparing his volume of poems for the press. Of these he read me two or three. . . . I guess the best philosophy will forthcome clearest in the poems. He is the first truly western poet, Óccidental as our forests and hills." Bronson, though he kept a copious journal, realized that he himself had more talent for the spoken than the written word. An account of his talks with Emerson, he felt certain, "would fill many pages, even had I the genius of transmitting it to paper. The best passages of life come often in conversation, and elude the catch of the pen." Bronson contented himself with building a summer house of willow wands cut from a nearby meadow: "Sweet is the toil and swift the hours glide by / When I my grounds delight to beautify." Here he would be the "happiest of men, to receive so happy a nature as this poet under a canopy made by my own hands." Henry Thoreau was, of course, a welcome visitor and helpful in a more ambitious project: a "lookout" on the hilltop. By climbing a tree he determined that "an ascent of 20 feet will give a wide prospect."

The year 1846 was memorable for other than Concord writers. The prolific Longfellow published *The Belfry of Bruges* and put the finishing touches on his vastly popular *Evangeline: A Tale of Arcadie.* John Greenleaf Whittier, Quaker poet of the abolitionist movement, brought out his embattled volume *Voices of Freedom.* Twenty-seven-year-old Herman Melville, who had returned two years earlier from his wanderings in the South Pacific, published his first book, *Typee,* which Hawthorne reviewed for the *Salem Advertiser,* saying that he liked it "uncommonly well." And Bronson Alcott read it in December with delight, characteristically seeing only the sunny side of that haunting tale. "A charming volume," he wrote in his journal, "as attractive even as *Robinson Crusoe.* I almost found myself embarked to spend the rest of my days with those simple islanders of the South Seas."

CHAPTER XI

WHAT THEY WERE READING

There is always room and occasion enough for a true book on any subject, as there is room for more light on the brightest day, and more rays will not interfere with the first.

—Henry D. Thoreau, *Journal*

Above: Engraving in *Graham's Magazine* (From *A History of American Magazines* by Frank Luther Mott)

IN 1846, CONCORD readers had access to plenty of "honestly American" literature in addition to Hawthorne's *Mosses*. Hawthorne himself had spent many afternoons reading in the Concord Athenaeum, which had been founded by Emerson, Thoreau, and others the same year that he and Sophia had come to town and which was housed in the vestry of the First Parish Church.* But the chief source of books for the population as a whole was the Social Library. Now twenty-five years old, it had grown out of the earlier Charitable Library, a collection of serious and conservative volumes stored in the home of the secretary. The Social Library offered both a wider choice of current literature and a more convenient location: Albert Stacy's general store in the center of town. Its shelves were filled with books of a very different sort from the weighty volumes of earlier days. Serious reading was still seen as a social good, as well as a practical tool for self-improvement; a well-read person could make an intelligent contribution to a democratic society, while improving his or her social position in the community. But the Social Library was no longer dominated by works on religion, politics, and moral instruction. Collections of old sermons, such as those Nathaniel Hawthorne had found in the attic of the Old Manse, if not yet "de-accessed," were gathering dust.

Whereas formerly the great majority of books had been the

*Thoreau had joined Emerson in donating subscriptions to the *London Phalanx*, the *Cambridge Miscellany*, the *Dial*, the *New York Weekly Tribune*, the *Anti-Slavery Standard*, the *Albany Cultivator*, the *Lynn Washingtonian*, and the *Boston Miscellany*.

work of European—largely English—authors, now American writers were widely read, especially those like James Fenimore Cooper, Washington Irving, Catherine M. Sedgwick, and Emerson's contemporary, Lydia Maria Child, all of whom romanticized the American past. Earlier generations, brought up in the Puritan tradition, had considered novels corrupting and invitations to sloth. Smollett and Fielding, for example, were thought to have low moral tone; they could be found only in private homes, not in public libraries. But Sir Walter Scott, with his vastly popular historical romances, had almost single-handedly given the novel a different image. Squire Hoar, for instance, had originally forbidden members of the family to read works of fiction. But one day, by happy accident, he found himself snowbound in a tavern with nothing to read but the first volume of *Red Gauntlet*. It was a revelation. He promptly subscribed to a complete set of the *Waverly Novels*. In America, Cooper had achieved a spectacular success with his romantic novels of the now-vanishing frontier. Concord readers in 1846 had no less than seven of his books to choose from, each of which had become the best-seller for its year of publication. By midcentury, fiction was the largest single category in the Social Library's collection.

Few Concord readers could have been unaware that something exciting was going on in literary circles. In Cambridge and elsewhere, young writers—most of them younger than Emerson—were building national reputations. Henry Wadsworth Longfellow, a Bowdoin classmate of Nathaniel Hawthorne, was now professor of modern languages at Harvard, living in the Craigie House on Brattle Street (the Vassell House of Edmund Hosmer's Tory grandmother). Longfellow had already won a reputation as a popular poet as well as a scholar. Oliver Wendell Holmes brought out two books during the year: *Urania* and a book of *Poems*. James Russell Lowell, Harvard's Class Poet in 1838, had already produced two volumes of verse. John Greenleaf Whittier's *Voices of Freeman* was making an eloquent contribution to the anti-slavery movement. Edgar Allan Poe's *The Raven and Other Poems*, which had only recently appeared, was already on the road to becoming a best-seller.

American history was being read avidly, as perhaps never before. Although the *Concord Freeman* may have been stretching a point in comparing the ragtag army invading Texas with Cortés and the conquerors of Montezuma, William H. Prescott's *History of the Conquest of Mexico*, published only three years earlier, was exceedingly well timed. George Bancroft was well started on his monumental *History of the United States*, a ten-volume work embodying the aggressive nationalism characteristic of an era of expansion. In Cambridge, Jared Sparks was busily engaged in editing the writings of George Washington and Benjamin Franklin.

Meanwhile, books from Britain, though no longer dominant, were more than holding their own. Emerson and Thoreau were not alone in their enthusiasm for Thomas Carlyle. His book *On Heroes and Hero-Worship* was all the rage in American intellectual circles (and was, unfortunately, supporting the theory of a "superior" race). Concord readers had plenty of English authors to choose from. Charles Dickens, of course, led the list—which included Tennyson, DeQuincy, Bulwer-Lytton, and, most recently, Benjamin Disraeli, with his novel *Coningsby*. Jane Austen, long after her death, was slowly gaining recognition on this side of the Atlantic. Anthony Trollope was just embarking on his career, but his mother, Frances Trollope, had broken open a hornet's nest with her acerbic *Domestic Manners of the Americans*, which was widely read with indignation and perhaps with a certain masochistic pleasure. In a recently published volume, George Palmer Putnam had sought to correct Mrs. Trollope's false impressions of American cultural life. Although his defense did not have the popular appeal of her attack, his title alone promised to demolish his adversary: *American Facts, Notes and Statistics, Relative to the Government, Resources, Manufacturers, Commerce, Religion, Education, Literature, Fine Arts, Manners and Customs of the United States of America.*

Among French writers, two of the most famous were being read over here: Victor Hugo and Alexandre Dumas—both close contemporaries of Emerson. *The Hunchback of Notre Dame* had been published in America the same year that Emerson moved to Concord. And in 1846 Dumas was at the height of his powers. *The Three Musketeers* and *The Count of Monte Cristo* had appeared during the preceding two years and won instant popularity. (When he sailed for Europe in 1847, Emerson found Dumas's novels in the little ship's library.)

On November 6, 1846, the *Concord Freeman* printed the first installment of *Dombey and Son,* by Charles Dickens. Exactly ten years earlier, Dickens had been published for the first time in America: a small green volume containing the first four numbers of *Pickwick*. By 1842, when he made his first American visit and lecture tour, Dickens had become a national idol. Publishers here vied with one another in printing each novel—published serially, in installments called parts—as soon as they could get sheets from England. Prices were low, since in most cases the books were pirated; that is, no royalties were paid to the author, whose work was not protected by American copyright. Wiley and Putnam in New York (the same company that had published Hawthorne's *Mosses*) sold *Dombey* for one American shilling (twelve cents) per part; another publisher, in Philadelphia, charged only six cents. This situation was fine for American readers but irksome for foreign writers living on their royalties. The pirating of his novels—together with his loathing for slavery and for many of our country's domestic habits—soured Dickens's response to the American scene: "I trust," he wrote, "never to see the Mississippi again except in dreams and nightmares." His abusive *American Notes* aroused a storm of criticism—and sold all the better for that. But Emerson was not impressed. "Yesterday I read Dickens's *American Notes,*" he wrote in his journal. "It answers its end very well, which plainly was to make a readable book, nothing more. Truth is not his object for a single instant." Emerson was no better pleased with Dickens's novels, which his friends had praised so highly: "[Dickens's] eye rests always on surfaces; he has no insight into Character. . . . Like Cooper and Hawthorne he has no dramatic talent. The moment he attempts dialogue the improbability of life hardens to wood and stone." When *Dombey and Son* began appearing in the *Freeman,* Waldo doubtless passed it up.

While English and American writers were competing for the American market, a very different sort of competition was going on: a battle over the language itself. In 1846, Concord readers had the choice of two dictionaries: Noah Webster's *American Dictionary of the English Language* and Joseph Worcester's *Comprehensive and Explanatory Dictionary of the English Language.* Webster, whose dictionary had recently been revised and enlarged, was determined to establish an American language, free from slavish imitation of English spelling and usage. Worcester (who, incidentally, was living in Craigie House when Longfellow took rooms there) held uncompromisingly to orthodox British spelling and pronunciation. The leading New England writers were on his side. Oliver Wendell Holmes referred to "Mr. Worcester's Dictionary, on which, as is well known, the literary men of this metropolis are by special statute allowed to be sworn in place of the Bible."

Webster sued Worcester for plagiarism, thus initiating the so-called War of Dictionaries. Actually, it was a contest for the American market. In the long run, Webster won hands down.

As library records show, Concordians in midcentury were enthusiastic readers. But Emerson's reading habits seem beyond belief. His son Edward, in editing Waldo's journals, listed the writers quoted from or referred to during the year 1846. Many of the names are reasonably familiar: Pindar, Anacreon, Copernicus, Roger Bacon, Spenser, Chapman, Kepler, Donne, Defoe, Cowper, Kant, Burke, Goethe, Burns, Robert Owen, Fourier, Carlyle, Webster, Everett, Alcott, Bryant, Tennyson, Dickens, Longfellow, Elizabeth Barrett, Robert Browning. But how about Drelincourt, Pons de Capdueil, Schleiermacher, Von Hammer-Purgstall (who translated Hafiz), and O. MacKnight Mitchell (author of *Planetary and Stellar Worlds*)? And there were many more.

If by midcentury the number of books Concord residents had to choose from was impressive, the number of magazines they might subscribe to was staggering. These ranged from the *North American Review,* voice of the literary establishment, to a hoard of popular journals, some of which died within a few years of publication. The year 1846 alone saw the birth of no less than fourteen new magazines, in New York City, Boston, Albany, Pittsburgh, Cincinnati, Baltimore, and New Orleans. Many publications in these years were devoted to "self-improvement," that is, to the wider dissemination of knowledge through all levels of society, made possible by the availability of cheap paper and improved printing presses. New periodicals specialized in law, medicine, music, drama, education, science (*Scientific American* was founded in 1845), religion (of all denominations), agriculture, mechanics, politics, phrenology, fashion—in every conceivable subject. Literary journals abounded. Others—notably the distinguished and long-lived *Youth's Companion*—catered to young readers. But the real money, the big sales, were to be found in the highly competitive popular magazines, with their romantic stories and pretty poems, their cautionary tales and edifying advice, their household hints and illustrations of the latest fashions. They were aimed at the family market: principally at the fair sex, the heart of the home.

How many of these family magazines were read by the women of Concord is not recorded. But one we can take for granted. Entitled *Godey's Lady's Book,* it was the brainchild of a plump, benign, very shrewd businessman of Philadelphia named Louis A. Godey, who boasted that "from Maine to the Rocky Mountains there is scarcely a hamlet, however inconsiderable, where [the magazine] is not received and read, and, in the larger towns and cities, it is universally distributed." His purpose was "to bring unalloyed pleasure to the female mind. . . . Nothing having the slightest appearance of indelicacy shall ever be admitted to the *Lady's Book*."

By claiming readership west to the Rocky Mountains, where the population consisted largely of Indians and an occasional fur trader, Godey may have been stretching a point. Yet by midcentury, circulation was in the thirty thousands (an amazing figure for the time) and still growing. Concord's interest in the *Lady's Book* must surely have increased when Godey acquired the *Ladies' Magazine* of Boston, together with its editor, Mrs. Sarah Josepha Hale, a high-minded, competent widow who managed to print serious articles while purveying the sort of sentimentality that attracted subscribers and made for sales. A lady's magazine, to be sure, but what young man could resist the promise of her prospectus? "The lover will no longer," Hale wrote, "when bidding adieu to the 'lady of his love,' request her to gaze on that inconstant thing, the moon, so often obscured by clouds, and then remember her vows. He will present her his subscription for the *Ladies' Magazine;* and the sweet smile with which the gift is received will recur, like a dream of light to his memory, while reflecting that the soft eyes of his charmer, are, for *his sake,* often employed on its pure pages."

Mrs. Hale herself wrote fiction, essays, and popular verse, of which "Mary Had a Little Lamb. . ." proved the most enduring. She gave more weight to *Godey's* by continuing to promote such causes as women's education, including learning the practice of medicine so that a woman could become a "doctoress." Louis Godey, however, avoided publishing articles on economic and social issues, viewing them as unsuitable for the female mind. (There was no mention, for example, of the antislavery movement.) As for politics, one did not mention the subject in a lady's presence without asking her pardon. Yet Sarah Hale did succeed in opening the magazine to serious writers. Emerson, Hawthorne, Longfellow, Holmes, and Harriet Beecher Stowe all contributed.

The most sensational issue of *Godey's Lady's Book* appeared in May 1846. It contained the first installment of a scathing series entitled "The New York Literati" by the country's best-known and most acerbic literary critic, Edgar Allan Poe. Many readers, as well as writers, found it offensive. Not wholly to Godey's surprise, the issue was quickly sold out and had to be reprinted. He piously disclaimed any blame for hurt feelings, maintaining that these were "Mr. Poe's opinions, not our own."

Poe's hostility toward established writers was already well

known in Concord. Only the previous year his half-drunken lecture in Boston had caused something of a literary scandal. Some months earlier he had published a series of articles accusing Longfellow (his principal bête noire) and other contemporary authors of plagiarism. The new series was directed toward New York writers and editors who cynically puffed up one another's work no matter what they really thought of it, writers who, said Poe, could not construct "three successive sentences in grammatical English." By contrast, he did refer briefly to Hawthorne as an extraordinary genius who had failed to gain wide recognition because he was too poor to buy favors from the reviewers (a rather backhanded compliment).

Hawthorne's own view of Poe was ambivalent. When *Mosses from an Old Manse* came on the market in early June of 1846, he instructed his publishers to send Poe a copy for review and followed this gesture with a personal letter to the critic himself. After expressing his satisfaction with Poe's favorable notices of earlier work, Hawthorne went on to say that he cared "for nothing but the truth; and shall always much more readily accept a harsh truth, in regard to my writings, than a sugared falsehood." He need not have worried—particularly since he concluded by confessing that "I admire you rather as a writer of tales than as a critic upon them."*

Emerson that summer was busy with his own affairs, which included preparing for publication of his first book of poems. Although he had not been personally attacked by Poe, the latter had consistently ridiculed the transcendentalists and

*More than a year later, in a critical essay, Poe would advise Hawthorne to "mend his pen, get a bottle of visible ink, come out from the Old Manse, cut Mr. Alcott, hang (if possible) the editor of the *Dial,* and throw out of the window to the pigs all his odd numbers of *The North American Review.*"

their magazine, the *Dial.* Poe did concede that Emerson's "love of the obscure does not prevent him . . . from the composition of occasional poems in which beauty is apparent *by flashes.*" Waldo doubtless had in mind Poe's new book, *The Raven and Other Poems,* when he termed the author "the jingle-man"—an additional reason, perhaps, for his turning down a New York publisher's offer to bring out his own work as a companion volume to Poe's.

Godey's Lady's Book may be as good a choice as any to suggest the sort of popular-magazine material available to the people of Concord at that time. Literary criticism like the Poe series was the exception. The standard fare was the sentimental story, invariably pointing a moral; characters are pious, insufferably righteous. There were light essays on music and the arts, on beauty and health and female fashions (the latter ironically illustrated with drawings of wasp-waisted women whose health was obviously being endangered). And there was lots of poetry—or, at least, verse. Circulation rose steadily despite such unmannerly comments as that of Horace Greeley's recently founded New York *Tribune:* "The *Lady's Book* seems to us sadly misnamed, for it is of late uniformly filled with trash—the most unmeet offering in the world for those to whom it is addressed."

CHAPTER XII

SARAH AND ELIZABETH

Mrs. Ripley was known and revered in the region where she lived, as one who combined rare and living knowledge of literature and science with the household skill and habits of personal labor needful to New England women of limited means. . . . To the ordinary cares of her station were added those of assisting her husband in the cares of a boys' boarding school. . . . And amid all the activity of her busy life the love and habit of acquiring knowledge, which was the life of her age as of her ardent youth, kept even pace.

—Elizabeth Hoar, *Life of Mrs. Samuel Ripley*

Above: Sarah A. Ripley

For Emerson, one of the happiest events of 1846 was the return to Concord in April of Sarah and Samuel Ripley. After a long and successful ministry in Waltham, Ezra Ripley's son had retired to his childhood home in the Old Manse.

Sarah Alden Bradford Ripley, descendant of William Bradford and John Alden of Plymouth Plantation, was born in Boston in 1793. Early in life she had become a brilliant scholar in an age when, in the words of the father of one of her friends, "all knowledge, except that of domestic affairs, appears unbecoming in a female." Fortunately, her own father, a scholarly sea captain, had held more enlightened views. When Sarah's schoolmaster "asked one day if she would like to study Latin," recalled her friend Elizabeth Hoar, "it was a fortnight before she could make up her mind to ask her father's leave, but one day she came home and with great timidity said, 'Father, may I study Latin?' Her father laughed and exclaimed, 'A girl study Latin! Yes, study Latin if you want to. You may study anything you please.' "

Young Sarah was soon at home in both Latin and Greek. By the age of fourteen she was reading Voltaire's novels in the original French. She learned Italian and German (which she considered "an abominable language"), all this without the help of adequate dictionaries or well-edited editions of the classics. Nor was her zest for knowledge confined to languages. She studied mathematics and philosophy, chemistry and astronomy. Her greatest love was for botany: No other woman, said the famous botanist Asa Gray, could match her in that field.

Sarah had been close to the Emerson family for many years. She recalled her first encounter with Waldo's formidable and eccentric aunt, Mary Moody Emerson: "She heard of me when I was 16 years old as a person devoted to books and a sick mother, sought me out in my garret without an introduction, and though received at first with sufficient coldness, she did not give up until she had enchained me entirely in her magic circle." Mary recognized her young friend's talent when Sarah was still unsure of herself, nor was she put off by the precocious girl's independent spirit. "You are the only person who ever thought me of any consequence," Sarah wrote to Mary, "and I am pretty well convinced other folks are more than half right. I want you to love me, but you must do as you please about it."

Four years after their first meeting, Mary had recruited Sarah to assist in the education of eleven-year-old Waldo (only nine years her junior), following his father's untimely death. Soon Sarah had her pupil corresponding with her in Latin. It was the beginning of a remarkable friendship between two complex and very different personalities.

When, at her father's behest, Sarah became engaged to Mary's half-brother, Samuel Ripley, she warned Mary: "Your family have no idea what trouble they may be entailing on themselves. I make no promises of good behavior, but, knowing my tastes and habits, they must take the consequences upon themselves." Samuel was starting out on his career as minister of the Unitarian church in Waltham. And to supplement his modest salary, he and Sarah undertook to conduct a boarding school for boys in their home. Thus, Sarah assumed both the duties of a clergyman's wife and—far more to her liking—a schoolteacher.

While an undergraduate at Harvard, Waldo had spent vacations helping the Ripleys with their school. Being with Sarah, he felt, was quite as stimulating as listening to lectures by his Harvard professors. "At leisure moments you will find her reading a German critic or something of the kind, sometimes Reid on Light or Optics. As to her knowledge, talk on what you will and she can always give you a new idea—ask her any philosophical question, she will always enlighten you by her answer." Many years later, Emerson recalled Sarah's extraordinary learning as a young woman: "At a time when perhaps no other woman read Greek, she acquired the language with ease, and read Plato—adding soon the advantage of German commentators."

How Sarah found time to read Plato is hard to imagine. In addition to the strains of raising a large family (nine children, two of whom died in infancy), she had the main responsibility for running the boarding school. She was a born teacher—better, perhaps, than she knew. "I remember her now with the strongest feeling of reverence, affection and gratitude," wrote one of her pupils, Senator George Frisbie Hoar. "I do not think she ever knew how much her boys loved her." Teaching she enjoyed; not so her other duties. Though she claimed that she never regretted having given up "the independence of an attic covered with books for the responsibilities and perplexities of a parish and a family," rebellion lurked beneath the surface. In a moment of candor she wrote to a close friend, "I would there were any hole to creep out of this most servile of all situations, a country clergyman's wife. Oh, the insupportable fatigue of affected sympathy with ordinary and vulgar minds." No wonder that Sarah suffered from severe headaches throughout her married life.

It was a happy day—indeed a homecoming—when, freed at last from the trials and duties of a clergyman's wife (her husband having retired), Sarah moved with him into the Old

The Old Manse (Drawing by May Alcott)

Manse. "I wonder if my first experience of a morning in Concord can ever be repeated—the bright river which I welcomed as my own, the trees covered with chattering blackbirds, good as rooks, the feeling that I had at last a *home*." For her husband, Samuel, the move was a return to the one place on earth he most loved: "Every object—every chair and picture and table and tree—is dear to me." (Alas, Samuel was to enjoy the new life for less than two years. On the eve of Thanksgiving in 1847, he died suddenly as he was driving a group of children to his home for the next day's festivities. A tall, portly gentleman whose impetuous temperament and firm opinions sometimes concealed his warm heart, he had been a loyal benefactor of the Emerson boys ever since the early death of their father. "He was the hoop that held us all staunch," recalled Waldo, "with his sympathies of family and with that disinterestedness which we have hardly witnessed in any other person." As for Sarah, she would live on in the Old Manse for another twenty years, continuing her literary studies—she complained that she could not read Sanskrit without a dictionary!—and tutoring Harvard undergraduates who had been "conditioned" for failure in classical studies. Ties with Harvard had been strong ever since 1775, when the college buildings were requisitioned by the Continental army, and faculty and students had moved to Concord for the winter.)

By no stretch of the imagination can Sarah Ripley be seen as a typical woman of her time. Yet her life gives a hint of what such intellectual women were up against in the mid–nineteenth century. She had done her duty and had even convinced herself that she had no regrets. Maybe so. Yet it is hard to believe, considering that Professor Child of Harvard described her as "the most learned woman I have ever known" and that, in the opinion of President Edward Everett, she was a woman who could have filled any professor's chair in the college.

We can only speculate about what Sarah's influence might have been in a later era, when academic careers were open to women. One thing we do know: She had a lasting influence on Emerson—too much of an influence, according to Waldo's fiercely orthodox Aunt Mary. When Waldo published his first series of *Essays,* Mary had been horrified by "this strange medley of atheism and false independence" and blamed Sarah for "early infecting him with infidelity." It is indeed likely that, as Sarah's pupil and friend, Waldo had been "infected" with her independence of mind, her skeptical view of time-honored Puritan doctrine, and her personal belief in self-reliance. But she remained too realistic, too down-to-earth, to accept his persistent optimism or to follow him in his flights into the empyrean. She had fostered his spirit of independence; now she did what she could to keep his feet on the ground. One day when they were taking a walk together, Sarah had suggested that the soul's serenity was at best nothing more than resignation to what could not be helped. "Oh, no," Waldo replied, "not resignation. Aspiration is the soul's true state!" All very well for Waldo. More difficult, perhaps, for Sarah, who apparently aspired only to a quiet life in search of knowledge and truth but had accepted, with no outward protest, a more "becoming" career for a woman. Commenting on the portraits of Sarah in her later years, Gamaliel Bradford remarks that "her features are calm, thoughtful, noble, sympathetic, but with a hint of the sadness of one who has meditated long on life with vast comprehension and limited hope."

Elizabeth Hoar (By permission of the Ralph Waldo Emerson Memorial Association and of the Houghton Library)

* * *

" 'Elizabeth of Concord,' as I have called her," writes Elizabeth Maxfield-Miller, editor of Elizabeth Hoar's letters, "was an outstanding woman of nineteenth-century Concord, by her ancestry and family, by her very close association with the Emersons, and by her friendship from childhood to old age with famous men and women of Concord and of the Emerson circle at home and abroad. Like her dear older friend, Sarah Bradford Ripley of the Old Manse (whose biography she published in 1877), Elizabeth [Hoar] was an intellectual and a scholar as well as a warm-hearted human being."

The death of young Charles Emerson in 1836, only four months before he was to marry Elizabeth Hoar, had been almost as crushing a blow to Waldo as it had been to her. "In Charles," he declared, "I found society that indemnified me for almost total seclusion from all others." At the funeral, Waldo had been heard to lament, "When one has had but little society—and all that society is taken away—what is there to live for?" Only one person could—to some degree—take Charles's place. That was Elizabeth. Her brother later recalled that "until about 1846 [the year Sarah Ripley returned to Concord] Emerson had, I think, no intimate friend outside of his own household, except my sister Elizabeth, who had been betrothed to his brother Charles."

The Hoars and the Emersons had always been close. Waldo admired the Squire—whose austere uprightness reminded him of a Roman senator—and had been delighted when his brilliant young brother joined Sam Hoar's law office. Now, ten years after Charles's death, Sam's daughter Elizabeth was a member of the Emerson family in all but name. She had no intention of marrying; her goal was to live up to Charles's expectations, honor his memory through her own way of life. Waldo always thought of her as his sister. "Elizabeth Hoar consecrates," he wrote. "I have no other friend whom I more wish to be immortal than she; an influence I cannot spare, but must always have on hand for recourse." "Elizabeth the Wise" he called her, so impressed was he with her learning. Elizabeth, on her part, considered Waldo one of the great teachers of their time.

Maxfield-Miller has described Elizabeth's role in the Emerson household, saying that for Waldo, she was "an Egeria, a sister, a friend, a literary counselor, a secretary, and a general factotum." She was also a close companion (and apparently a ready helpmeet) to Lidian, "often taking over the management of the household, the servants, and the children during Lidian's frequent illnesses or her absence in Plymouth." Waldo's older brother William, a New York judge, and his wife, Sarah, were always delighted with Elizabeth's visits; their children, like Waldo and Lidian's, knew her as "Aunt Lizzie." Waldo's mother she addressed as "Dear Mama"; to Ruth she was like a long-cherished daughter-in-law. And Waldo's formidable, hard-to-please aunt, Mary Moody Emerson, had transferred the deep affection she had felt for Charles, her favorite nephew, to his fiancée, deluging Elizabeth with loving letters all the rest of her life.

Concord villagers were an independent-minded lot. But they could all agree on their affection for Elizabeth. Nathaniel Hawthorne, who had only recently left town, had good reason to be grateful to her. It was she who had urged her friend Sophia Peabody to settle in Concord. Coming straight to the Old Manse from the wedding, Nathaniel and Sophia had found the "musty edifice," vacant since the death of the venerable Ezra Ripley, brightened with flowers everywhere, arranged for their reception by Elizabeth—who, practical as always, had come, shyly, that first evening with a gift of freshly made butter. Nathaniel did not receive visitors gladly, but Elizabeth had always been welcome. "Elizabeth Hoar (who is much more at home among spirits than among fleshly bodies) came hither a few times, merely to welcome as us to the ethereal world," wrote Nathaniel, "but latterly she has vanished into some other region of infinite space." "There was a blessing in her presence," recalled Sophia. "She talked a great deal, gently, with a penetrating sweetness of voice, and looking somewhat down, as those do who have just received the news of a bitter sorrow. She knew everything that was fine in history and poetry and art; to be near her and to catch at moments the clear unfaltering challenge of her sad but brave eyes was to live a little nobler one's self."

Sophia may have been exaggerating her friend's knowledge. But the fact is that Elizabeth, like Sarah Ripley and Margaret Fuller, had, for a woman in those times, been remarkably well educated since childhood. Her father, who recognized a bright girl when he saw one, had started her studying the classics at the age of seven. She had taken Greek lessons with Ezra Ripley and had remained a Greek scholar all her life. At Concord Academy—of which her father was a founder—Elizabeth had been a schoolmate of Henry Thoreau and of her brother Rockwood. Later she had become an intimate friend of both Margaret Fuller and of Margaret's younger sister Ellen, wife of Ellery Channing. Elizabeth had attended Margaret's famous "Conversations"* in Boston and

*Annie Sawyer Downs, in her *Memoirs,* wrote: "Some of the Concord ladies, however, did not appreciate Miss Fuller's fine sentiments, among whom it is odd now to remember were the two maiden aunts of Mr. Henry Thoreau. 'All bosh, my dear!' exclaimed Miss Maria Thoreau to a disappointed matron whom domestic duties kept away from a much anticipated conversation,—'when a woman does not know herself what she wants to say, how can she expect anybody else to find out?' "

been one of the few women invited to meetings of the distinguished (but short-lived) Transcendental Club.

Elizabeth's relationship with Henry Thoreau was more complex. Though they had gone to school together, she was never completely at ease with him in later life. "I love Henry," she once remarked, "but do not like him." He was shy and stiff with women. One of the Emersons' serving girls noticed that he never went through the kitchen without coloring, while Elizabeth said that, as for taking his arm, she would as soon think of taking the arm of an elm tree. (She modified this opinion when she got to know him better through the Emerson family.)

No one admired Elizabeth more than young, handsome George William Curtis who, with his brother Burrill, had so charmed the company at Brook Farm. In the early summer of 1846, George was boarding in Concord for the third time but planning soon to leave town. He wrote to his friend and former Brook Farmer, John S. Dwight: "I feel a pang in going to-night to take leave of Elizabeth Hoar, who is going away for several weeks, and who will not return until I have left Concord. She seems to me one who may at any moment become invisible, like a pure flame."

Elizabeth departed on June 6 initially to visit the William Emersons in New York and later to stay with cousins in New Haven. A chatty letter written to Waldo during her absence shows her as less ethereal than Curtis and the Hawthornes had depicted her:

New Haven July 29th [1846]

Dear Waldo

I have told mother I should probably go home Saturday of this week. & now I wish to tell her that I shall not be home till the Saturday following. Will you forgive me that I address [this] brief letter to you instead of her that I may tell you how welcome was the sight of your handwriting, any the least sign from you or yours, of whom no syllable has reached me since I parted from you at the Concord Depot. If you had remembered how easily children are pleased, you would have been more willing to write the letter, but after reading it, I was sorry to have annoyed you by asking for it.—There is nothing in this New Haven life to make a story out of. It is beautifully green in the beautiful avenue, showers fall daily, the East & West Rock overlook the leafy city, themselves crowned & garlanded with dense green foliage, flowers abound in the parlours & gardens, well-dressed young ladies flit through the streets, cool summer fairies, courteous young gentlemen of tender age bring them water-lilies, escort them to lectures & home from parties, of which chivalrous attentions, mixed with deference due to age, I receive my share. We ride, we receive calls, we return them in due season, hear Mr. Hudson's lectures,* we criticise the lecturer, we read Shakespeare & Mosses from an Old Manse, we answer enquiries about R. W. Emerson, & Hawthorne & Margaret Fuller (God bless her). . . . But "I weary of details" as well as Aunt Mary & her nephews, so if my dear though erring brother Waldo will give my love & best wishes to his & my dearest mamma, to Lidian & her babies, to George & the Ripleys, to all who ask for it, if any;—I will go & make the isinglass jelly for the said party, & hope to do myself honour in the result; After which I will return to the peaceful meadows of Concord, & if I can find any body left to love me, will warm myself by that fire through the coming winter, otherwise I will take to the study of physical science, or perhaps to "lithographic drawing."

Farewell ω!δαιμοιε φεριστε [O godlike bravest one]
Your sister E.

As Elizabeth was well aware, she need not have worried about finding anybody left to love her when she returned to the peaceful meadows of Concord. Who did not? Yet a comment by Mary Hosmer Brown reminds one of Gamaliel Bradford's sensitive response to portraits of Sarah Ripley: "The lovely Elizabeth Hoar was always much beloved by Mr. Em-

*Henry Norman Hudson had lectured at the Concord Lyceum the previous year.

erson as the fiancée of his brother. When I knew her years after Charles Emerson's death, a slight atmosphere of sadness clung to her, like a delicate perfume. She used to say that she must live the most beautiful life she could, or Charles might get way ahead of her."

CHAPTER XIII

WOMEN IN A MAN'S WORLD

The whole education of women ought to be relative to men. To please them, to be useful to them, to make themselves loved and honored by them, to educate them when young, to care for them when grown, to counsel them, to console them, and to make life sweet and agreeable to them—these are the duties of women at all times and what should be taught them from their infancy.

—Jean-Jacques Rousseau

Above: Margaret Fuller

SARAH RIPLEY'S SENSE of resignation, her acceptance—however reluctant—of a woman's station in life, failed to satisfy certain of her more aggressive contemporaries. While Sarah was busy raising a family and teaching in her husband's school, two Massachusetts women born the same year (1793) were passionately engaged in bettering the education and social position of their sex, in fighting discrimination at all levels of society. One of them, Lucretia Mott, a gentle, soft-spoken Quaker from Nantucket with a will of iron, had become widely known as the founder of the first Female Anti-Slavery Society and an outspoken advocate of women's rights. (These two causes were closely allied.) The other, Mary Lyon, the precocious daughter in a farm family of western Massachusetts, had persuaded a group of businessmen and ministers to sponsor a fund drive for a new sort of educational institution for women, one in which women would learn to be more than homemakers and schoolteachers. Mary Lyon's sponsors expected her to be self-effacing. "It is desirable," she wrote to a colleague, "that the plans relating to the subject should not seem to originate with *us* but with benevolent *gentlemen*." Otherwise "many good men will fear the effect on society of so much female influence." But though it was deemed unladylike to travel alone and speak in public, she eventually had to raise most of the money herself. The result was Mount Holyoke Female Seminary, which, by 1846, had been in operation for nine years, establishing a new era in women's education.

Meanwhile, in Vermont a schoolteacher named Emma Hart Willard, married to the head of an academy for boys and a lover of learning for its own sake, was creating new teaching methods suggestive of what would someday be known as progressive education. This approach had its hazards. When she established the Troy Female Seminary in upper New York State, visiting parents were horrified to find pupils in a physiology class drawing diagrams of the human body. Thereafter, "to preserve the modesty of the girls and spare them too frequent agitation," heavy paper was posted over such illustrations in their textbooks. Later on, Mrs. Willard (who won respect for her educational methods despite such parental reactions) founded an association for the Mutual Improvement of Female Teachers—most of whom had only rudimentary schooling themselves and could not command salaries remotely comparable to college-trained men.

Most offensive of all to the establishment, to the accepted view of women's place in society, were those who overstepped the bounds of propriety by espousing political causes like the abolition of slavery and—worst of all—had the effrontery to address large public meetings. Outstanding among these activists were the Grimké sisters, courageous abolitionists from the South who had been speaking to enthusiastic audiences in Boston and in towns throughout New England. Opposition to them had come largely from the Congregational church. A pastoral letter drew attention to "the dangers which at present seem to threaten the female character with widespread and permanent injury. The appropriate duties and influence of women are clearly stated in the New Testament. . . . The power of women is her dependence, flowing from the consciousness of that weakness which God has given her for her protection." Concord parishioners held other views. When the Grimkés came to town, Lidian Emerson was one of the hostesses who welcomed them. And soon after their departure, Waldo gave an address on slavery in the Concord church. Yet a brief unrelated entry in his journal during this period oddly echoes the Congregational ministers' comment on the source of women's power: "A woman's strength is not masculine, but is the unresistible strength of weakness."

In 1846, Concord certainly had its fair share of intelligent women. Yet their male counterparts, however sensitive and articulate, accepted the conventional wisdom of their time about a woman's mental capacity and proper role in society.

Waldo admired and respected Sarah Ripley, but he obviously considered her exceptional, virtually unique: "How rarely can a female mind be impersonal. Sarah R. is wonderfully free from egotism of place and time and blood." His occasional brief comments on the subject of women are revealing because they are so casual—mere illustrations of a truth he took for granted. In his lecture on "Uses of Great Men" (delivered in April of 1846 at the Concord Lyceum), he remarked on how we learn wisdom from men of genius almost without effort, "as a wife arrives at the intellectual and moral elevations of her husband." Some years earlier he had jotted down in his journal his idea of women's role in life: "Woman should not be expected to write, or fight, or build, or compose scores; she does all by inspiring man to do all." Theoretically he believed in women's rights, but he deplored aggressive means of achieving them. "The things to be agitated for do not seem to me the best." By midcentury, however, he was willing to grant women the right to own property and to hold public office: "Whilst I should note thus, if women asked, or if men denied these things I should not wish women to wish political functions, nor, if granted assume them."

Waldo's young friend and erstwhile disciple Henry Thoreau, though no misognynist, underrated women's intelligence; he avoided their lectures (with the exception of those by Margaret Fuller) because he felt women had nothing to say. Waldo's aunt Mary Moody Emerson he respected and admired because she appeared to have the intellect of a man. "She can entertain a large thought with hospitality, and is not prevented by any intellectuality in it, as women commonly are. In short, she is a genius, as woman seldom is, reminding you less often of her sex than any woman whom I know. . . . [S]he is capable of a masculine appreciation of philosophy and poetry." Best of all, he noted, she was a good listener: "More surely than any woman, [she] gives her companion occasion to utter his best thought."

Thoreau could be dogmatic about the assumed difference in intellect between the sexes. But not so when he sought to comprehend the mystery of sex itself. On May 5, 1846, he confided to his journal his private wrestlings with this elusive aspect of life:

> The subject of sex is a most remarkable one—since though it occupies the thoughts of all so much, and our lives & characters are so affected by the consequences which spring from this source—Yet mankind as it were tacitly agrees to be silent about it—at least the sexes do one to another. Here is the most interesting of all human facts or relations still veiled, more completely than the Eleusinian mystery—Out of such secresy [*sic*] & awe one would think that some religion would spring. I am not sorry for the silence—It is a golden reserve which speech has not yet desecrated—I believe it is unusual for the most intimate friends to impart the pleasures—or the anxieties connected with this fact—This is wonderfully singular—& when from this soil our flowers grow and music has its root here.
>
> I love men with the same distinction that I love woman—as if my friend were of some third sex—some other or stranger and still my friend.
>
> I do not think the Shakers exaggerate this fact—but all mankind exaggerate it much more by silence. In the true and noblest relations of the sexes there is somewhat akin to the secret of all beauty & art in the universe. The imagination of the Greeks filled the heavens full

of love & benignity in a thousand forms—flitting from this side to that—From Apollo in the sun to Aurora in the morning—still charming the world with this inexplicable variety—What sort of Dualism or difference there is who ever conceived? If there are Gods there are Goddesses Apollo & Venus—Neptune & Ceres—And the Hebrew's God is Love too.

What the difference is between man and woman—that they should be so attracted to one another I never saw adequately stated.

Bronson Alcott, whose interest in members of the female sex of all ages was vastly different from Thoreau's, nevertheless struck the same note when it came to mental capacity. His greatest compliment to a woman was that, though inspired by a woman's heart, she should have the intellect of a man.

Bronson's wife, Abby, would have none of this nonsense. Outwardly she kept quiet, but on occasion she let off steam in her journal:

> Wherever I turn I see the yoke on woman in some form or other—On some it sits easy for they are but beasts of burden, on others pride hushes them to silence—no complaint is made for they scorn pity or sympathy—on some it galls and chafes, they feel assured by every instinct of their nature that they were designed for a higher, nobler calling than to '*drag* life's lengthening chain along'—A woman may perform the most disinterested duties. She may '*die daily*' in the cause of truth and righteousness, she lives neglected [and] dies forgotten—But a man who never performed in his whole life one self-denying act, but who [has] accidentally gifts of Genius is celebrated by his contemporaries, while his name and his works live on, from age to age—he is crowned with Laurel while scarce a stone may tell where *She* lies.

And what of Nathaniel Hawthorne, who had only recently left the Old Manse, the Garden of Eden that he and Sophia had inhabited for the past three years? Soon after their wedding, Sophia had written to her mother, "There was never such a husband to enrich the world since it sprang out of

Drawing by May Alcott

chaos. I feel precisely like an Eve in Paradise." But an Eve who knew her place. Invariably tender and loving, Nathaniel treated Sophia as one might treat a very dear—if somewhat retarded—child. "Were you an angel," he wrote to her, "however holy and wise to come and dwell with mortals, he [angels are male, of course] would need the guidance and instruction of some mortal; and so will you, my Dove, need mine." In her journal, Sophia recorded one of their apparently rare quarrels, which occurred while they were on a walk in the woods. When she started to take a shortcut home through an unmowed hay field, he tried in vain to stop her, doubtless aware—as this city-bred girl was not—of the owner's feeling at having his hay trodden down. But reconciliation was swift: "I clasped him in my arms in the lovely shade. . . . Oh, how sweet it was! And I told him I would not be so naughty again!" Sophia's promise would have pleased the author of a tract entitled "The Cult of True Womanhood," who admonished her readers: "Oh, young and lovely bride, watch well the first moments when your will conflicts with his to whom God and society have given the control."

"In his relationships with women generally," writes Paula Blanchard in her life of Margaret Fuller, "Hawthorne is an extreme example of the prevailing attitudes of his time, attitudes which he shared with Timothy Fuller, James Freeman Clarke, Theodore Parker, and sometimes (though he would deny it) Ralph Waldo Emerson. He would not gainsay, in theory, a woman's right to be all she could be. But personally he expected women to be pretty, sensitive, silent, passive, and spiritually 'higher' than men, because altogether sexless."

Women were also expected to be physically frail. When Nathaniel first met Sophia, youngest of the three Peabody sisters, she had been living for some years as a semi-invalid in the family home, under the influence of an over-protective mother who had always treated her as a delicate child. Sophia suffered from persistent migraine headaches, for which physicians had prescribed one deadly drug after another, including mercury, arsenic, and opium. Though the drugs did not kill her, they did nothing to alleviate what she referred to as her "silent ministry of pain." The eventual cure was not drugs but the love of a handsome and devoted young man. By the time she and Nathaniel had married and moved into the Old Manse, Sophia was no longer an invalid.

This cult of female frailty was well publicized in the life of Elizabeth Barrett, who, on September 12, 1846, was secretly married to Robert Browning. Two years earlier, Harriet Martineau had written *Life in the Sick-room,* dedicated to "To—," assuming that Miss Barrett would know who was meant. Emerson was amused by the whole business. On November 7 he wrote to his friend Frederic Henry Hedge: "I found in town yesterday a precious piece of gossip from London; that 'Bells & Pomegranates' is engaged to 'Seraphine' or Miss Barrett; who is, the *divine bed-rid,* to whom Miss Martineau's 'Invalid' book was dedicated."

Among Hawthorne's female acquaintances, no one was more different from gentle, unassertive Sophia than the intelligent, strong-minded woman whom Nathaniel had come to know at Brook Farm and whom he would later lampoon in his novel *The Blithdale Romance.* Although, in his preface, he disclaimed any relationship between his fictional characters and real-life acquaintances, Margaret Fuller was surely the principal model for Zenobia, the "high-spirited Woman, bruising herself against the narrow limitations of her sex." In Nathaniel's view, such a woman was compensating for some lack, sexual or otherwise, in her private life.

Never a resident of Concord, Margaret had, by 1846, been closely associated with the intellectual life of the town for a decade. She had become a frequent visitor, thanks originally to her admiration for Emerson, with whom she had resided for weeks at a time. She had stayed with the Hawthornes and with her sister Ellen, wife of Ellery Channing. She had been closely associated with Bronson Alcott, when she succeeded Elizabeth Peabody as his assistant at the Temple School in Boston. "I wish it were my lot to see [her] much oftener," Bronson wrote to Charles Lane in January 1846, when she and Lane were both in New York, "for of women I know of none who fills a place more worthily. Most are quite out of place, if indeed there be place yet for them in the eye or heart of mankind." Even Henry Thoreau considered Margaret that rarity: a woman worth listening to. Her journal of a trip to the northwest wilderness, entitled *Summer on the Lakes,* had encouraged him to undertake his first, similarly discursive, book, *A Week on the Concord and Merrimack Rivers.*

Margaret Fuller's intellectual eminence, which was a source of wonder—and sometimes irritation—to her Concord acquaintances, had been achieved at a price. Born in Cambridge, brought up under the affectionate but stern eye of a dominant father, she had from early childhood been subjected to the sort of rigorous education customarily given only to boys. Unlike Sarah Ripley, who as a schoolchild felt obliged to ask her father's permission to study Latin, Margaret had no choice. At six she was memorizing Virgil, soon followed by Plutarch. She discovered Shakespeare for herself when she was eight—though forbidden such "frivolous" reading on the Sabbath. A regimen like this, continued throughout her youth, inevitably made her shy and awkward in society, in danger of being considered an intellectual prig.

Highly emotional and uncommonly outspoken, Margaret seemed somewhat overpowering on first acquaintance. When she finally managed to get an introduction to Emerson, he found her unprepossessing. "Her extreme plainness, [not all agreed on this]—a trick of incessantly opening and shutting her eyelid,—the nasal tone of her voice,—all repelled; and I said to myself, we shall never get far." But she soon won him over, and then some. This initial visit lasted three weeks. Margaret's relationship with Waldo and the transcendentalist group grew in strength over the years. She became the leading light in the "conversations" at Elizabeth Peabody's West Street bookstore. When the transcendentalist journal the *Dial* was founded, she took the (rather thankless) job of editor and did much of the writing. But it was as a talker and a teacher that she excelled. Emerson believed that her conversation was the most entertaining in America. And it always had an underlying purpose: to improve the status of women.

In early 1846, Margaret was living in New York City, busy writing articles for Horace Greeley's *Tribune* and preparing for the press a new book, *Papers on Literature and the Arts* (which included a comprehensive essay on the state of American literature) and also a second edition of her major work, *Woman in the Nineteenth Century,* which had been published the preceding year. This "essay" (as she called it) was an expansion of an earlier article entitled "The Great Lawsuit. Man versus Men: Woman versus Women." In her preface she explained that the previous title had been considered too obscure but that she preferred it for that very reason, "i.e. that it requires some thought to see what it means, and might thus prepare the reader to meet me on my own ground." Having issued this challenge, she proceeded with a somewhat rambling discourse, packed with learned references and literary quotations, amid which are many pungent passages on various aspects of a woman's plight, which she saw as inseparable from a man's. "By Man," she wrote, "I mean both man and woman. . . . The development of the one cannot be effected without that of the other." She rejected the idea that a woman, as a "profound thinker has said," belongs to her husband: "That is the very fault of marriage, and of the present relation between the sexes, that the woman does belong to the man, instead of forming a whole with him."

As for a woman's education, Margaret Fuller failed to share Rousseau's opinion that its sole object should be to make life sweet and agreeable for men. She had higher goals: "I would have woman lay aside all thought . . . of being taught and led by men. I would have her, like the Indian girl, dedicate herself to the Sun, the Sun of Truth, and go nowhere if his beams did not make clear the path." So with women's legal and political rights: It was time that men changed "their tone of feeling toward women as toward slaves." But nothing was likely to change until these rights were publicly represented by women.

While engaged in these literary pursuits, Margaret was at

the same time making plans to realize a lifelong ambition: to take an extended trip to Europe—to England, to France, and above all to Italy. Eleven years earlier, when she was twenty-five, she had been thrilled at the prospect of going abroad with friends; Europe she considered her spiritual home. But the opportunity was lost when her father suddenly died. Now she felt it was late but better than never. On August 1 she set sail from Boston.

(Shipwrecked and drowned on the return voyage four years later, she would never see her Concord friends again. Margaret Fuller was only forty years old when she died. But future historians would state that, during her brief life, she had "possessed more influence upon the thought of American women than any woman previous to her time.")

CHAPTER XIV

SEEING THE WORLD WITH NEW EYES

Could [America] transmute its social power into the higher forms of thought? Could it provide for the moral and intellectual needs of mankind? . . . Could it give new life to religion and art? Could it create and maintain in the mass of mankind those habits of mind which had hitherto belonged to men of science alone?

—Henry Adams, *History of the United States of America*

Above: Louis Agassiz (From *The Early Years of the Saturday Club* by Edward W. Emerson)

THE WIDESPREAD POPularity of the lyceums (there were literally thousands by 1846), the eagerness of book publishers to encourage local talent, reflected growing interest and pride in America's professional accomplishments in literature, in art, in science—in what could now be recognized as an American culture. The "honestly American" quality that critics found in Hawthorne's *Mosses from an Old Manse,* that Alcott recognized in Thoreau's *Week on the Concord and Merrimack Rivers,* and that Emerson expressed when he challenged his readers "to look at the world with new eyes" was equally clear in the progress of art and natural science. Landscape painters of the Hudson River School were establishing an American sense of identity. Lacking the picturesque past of the European scene, they found—as had Henry Thoreau—an even greater, more inspiring antiquity in our primeval forests, our rugged mountains, and, for a few, the vast expanses of the American West. Their work was closely associated with the rapid strides being made in the natural sciences. Artists were concerned that their pictures be true to the facts of nature. From the botanists they learned to depict authentic detail; they recognized a grand scheme of nature in the dramatic—if highly controversial—discoveries of the geologists. And always they shared the assumption that a supreme deity had planned it all.

The year 1846 was indeed a lively one for both natural science and technology, as some people in Concord were well aware. In the field of communication, 1846 saw both the invention of the rotary press and the coming of age of the telegraph, when the first line between New York and Washington went into operation. A landmark in the history of engineering, the world's first suspension bridge (spanning the Monongahela River) was reached that year, the work of a forty-year-old immigrant from Germany, John A. Roebling (later to become famous for his design of the Brooklyn Bridge). In the field of medicine, the year would be remembered for the first clinical use of ether by Doctors Morton and Warren at the Massachusetts General Hospital—a discovery in which Lidian Emerson's brother, Dr. Charles Jackson, was also involved. And for the future of American science as a whole—including the promotion of scientific literacy among the general public—probably the year's most significant event was the vote of Congress on August 10 that finally decided, after a decade of controversy, how best to use the bequest of an English aristocrat and scientist, James Smithson. He had left his estate "to the United States of America to found at Washington, under the name of the Smithsonian Institution, an establishment for the increase and diffusion of knowledge among men." Plans were made for a library and a national museum; and Dr. Joseph Henry, the professor at Princeton whose experiments in electromagnetism had made possible the invention of the telegraph, was appointed to direct what would become a worldwide center for research and education. Meanwhile, a major, multivolume work entitled *Cosmos,* by the great German naturalist Alexander von Humboldt, was currently in the process of being published. A year earlier Emerson had written in his journal: "*Cosmos*. The wonderful Humboldt, with his extended center, expanded wings, marches like an army, gathering all things as he goes. How he reaches from science to science, from law to law, tucking away moons and asteroids and solar systems, in the clauses and parentheses of his encyclopedical paragraphs!"

As Emerson's comment suggests, science had not yet

reached the stage of specialization; it still had an amateur quality in the best sense of that term. When members of the Harvard faculty formed the Scientific Club, it included not only professional scientists but lawyers, theologians, philosophers, and classicists, as well as the president of the college. The scientists themselves tended to be generalists. The botanist Asa Gray, for example, was the first American ever to hold a professorship exclusively in botany, and he saw himself as a zoologist as well. Gray, who had come to Harvard in 1842, was a practical scientist who would become well known to Concord intellectuals. But he had no interest whatever in the transcendental movement. Emerson, Thoreau, and Alcott meant little to him. What, one wonders, would he have made of Emerson's comment that "all science is transcendental, or else passes away. Botany is now acquiring a right theory. . . . The Avatars of Brahma will presently be textbooks of natural history." Nevertheless, as an upstate New Yorker, Gray was duly impressed by what he heard about New England women. Shortly after his arrival he wrote to a friend that he had heard about

> a learned lady in these parts, who assists her husband in his school, and who hears the boys' recitations in Greek and geometry at the ironing-board, while she is smoothing their shirts and jackets! reads German authors while she is stirring her pudding, and has a Hebrew book before her, when knitting. There's nothing like down East for learned women. Why, even the factory-girls at Lowell edit entirely a magazine, which an excellent judge told me has many better-written articles than the "North American Review." Vivent les femmes. There will be no use for men in this region, presently. Even my own occupation may soon be gone; for I am told that Mrs. Ripley (the learned lady aforesaid) is the best botanist of the country round.

Young Asa Gray's amusing comments about Sarah Ripley were literally true. With her thirst for knowledge wherever it was to be found, she was surely better equipped than most of her Concord friends to recognize the revolution in the natural sciences that was challenging traditional views of the world. Though Darwin's *Origin of Species* would not be published for another thirteen years, in 1846 the debate on the history of life on earth was already widespread and often bitter. Late in the year Asa Gray wrote, in the *North American Review,* a scathing attack on the anonymous author of a book on *Vestiges of the Natural History of Creation:* the work of an amateur scientist that, despite some fantastic theories, did suggest the evolution of species—a concept that Gray was not yet willing to accept and that many readers considered dangerous. (Emerson thought that everything in the book was good, "except the theology, which is civil, timid, and dull.") More important, the great and charming Swiss naturalist Louis Agassiz, newly arrived in America, delivered in the autumn the first of his "Lowell Lectures." Soon he would be revolutionizing the teaching of science at Harvard, where (as Edward Emerson later put it) "the government of the College rather regarded the Scientific and Medical Schools as an impertinence." Agassiz, who first appeared to Waldo Emerson as "a broad-featured unctuous man, fat and plenteous as some successful politician," would become the idol of lecture audiences.

Thanks to Agassiz and the work of geologists like the famous Sir Charles Lyell (whose *Travels in North America* had recently come on the market), it was clear that life on earth was a good deal older than the Old Testament implied. But this change from biblical to geological time did not shake the universal belief in divine providence; "a species," said Agassiz, "is a thought of the Creator." Like Agassiz, Asa Gray believed in special creation, by the direct agency of the Deity.*

*Many years later these two friends and colleagues would have a tragic falling-out, over Agassiz's refusal to accept Darwin's theory of natural selection.

As for Emerson, he was content with the providential theory, though he had little patience with the whole discussion: "I say to Lidian that the composition of the *What* is of no importance compared with the *How*. The most tedious of all discourses are on the subject of the Supreme Being." In any case, natural history apart from human history meant little to Emerson. "The greatest delight that the fields and woods minister is the suggestion of an occult relation between man and the vegetable. . . . They nod to me, and I to them."

Drawing by May Alcott

For the people of Concord, for those who wrote as well as those who tilled the soil, constant awareness of the natural world was an essential part of life. It is fair to say that none of the Concord authors would have had quite the same outlook, the same values, had they spent their lives in a big city. Emerson found in nature an unfailing source of strength and inspiration. Not the little-known reaches of South America that fed the genius of Alexander Humboldt; not the cane-brakes of Louisiana or the windswept coasts of Labrador that inspired the dramatic paintings of John James Audubon.* The gentle slopes of Fairhaven Hill, the sluggish Musketaquid or Grassground River at its foot, were not to be compared with the lofty mountain ranges and roaring torrents of more rugged, untamed country. But in the pastoral landscape of Concord Emerson found the serenity he sought. Looking down on Fairhaven Bay with Henry Thoreau, watching the stars to the music of the hylas in the swamp, he felt no need for wilder landscapes. Concord would suffice.

What of Bronson Alcott? "The good Alcott," Carlyle termed him, "with his long, lean face and figure, with his grey worn temples and mild, radiant eyes; all bent on saving the world by a return to acorns and the golden age"—how did he react to the world of nature, to the disturbing discoveries of the scientists? "I love nature much but man more," he declared. Unlike Thoreau, Alcott was a gardener, rather than a lover of the wilderness, but in his journal for April 1846 he admitted that "a simpler and more healthy poesy is emblemed in the wood than in the garden. . . . When I was seeking a family haunt, the woods about this village had a great attraction, and unwillingly I yielded to the necessity of settling near the roadside and the shorn beauty of the field." No naturalist, Alcott never learned to name to birds of Concord, but he loved their songs. On the Fourth of July he remarked with fury on the "monstrous boys" who shot them for fun, on "the gunner's crack aiming death to these joyous songsters of the air and groves."

An ardent reader, Alcott seemed interested in everything

*His eyesight failing, Audubon painted his last picture in 1846.

that was going on in 1846, including new discoveries in science. Yet his interpretation of these discoveries is somewhat bizarre. In his journal for January he wrote: "Professor Faraday, I read, is about presenting some discoveries of his to the Royal Society on the relation of Electricity and Magnetism to Light. I venture the conjecture that the three are states of One Substance, and that this, by whatsoever name it shall be designated, is the *immediate* Breath of Life, the nexus of Spirit and matter."

As readers of "The Old Manse" (the opening chapter of *Mosses*) were well aware, Nathaniel Hawthorne had his own special view of nature. To be sure, he, like Bronson Alcott, took delight in his garden. "It was one of the most bewitching sights in the world to observe a hill of beans thrusting aside the soil, or a row of early peas just peeping forth sufficiently to trace a line of delicate green." Like Emerson, Hawthorne drew morals—if somewhat laboriously—from the natural world. He marveled that the beautiful and fragrant white pond lilies in the Concord River could spring from the same black mud as the "slimy eel and speckled frog," the same out of which "the yellow lily sucks its obscene life and noisome odor. Thus we see, too, in the world that some persons assimilate only what is ugly and evil from the same moral circumstances which supply good and beautiful results to the daily life of others." Hawthorne envied Thoreau's intimacy with the natural scene, saying that to hear Henry talk was "like hearing the wind among the boughs of a forest-tree." Hawthorne himself yearned for something he could never achieve: "Oh that I could run wild!—that is, that I could put myself into a true relation with nature." In fact, the relation he enjoyed the most was one removed from reality. Looking out over the river on a calm evening, he observed, "Each tree and rock, and every blade of grass is distinctly imaged, and, however unsightly in reality, assumes ideal beauty in the reflection." At sunset, "all the sky glows downward at our feet." And he wondered that this muddy stream could "glorify itself with so adequate a picture of the heaven above it. . . . Let it be a symbol that the earthiest human soul has an infinite spiritual capacity."

Whatever lessons for mankind Hawthorne may have found in the placid river on his doorstep, he well understood—and perhaps shared—the fear of the wild and the unknown felt by the first settlers in New England. The gentle, sunlit countryside of Concord may have nourished his spirit, but the haunted landscape of his romances derived less from the world about him than from his own dark dreams and tragic sense of life.

For Henry Thoreau, on the other hand, the world of nature had none of these dark overtones; rather, it was a source of light, of inspiration. Emerson was amazed by his young friend's knowledge of natural history. An avid amateur botanist, Henry claimed that he could tell the day of the year from what wildflowers were in bloom. But he never saw himself as a scientist. He abhorred museum collections of pickled specimens. "A man's interest in a single bluebird is worth more than a complete but dry list of the fauna and flora of a town." Yet he scorned "the mealy-mouthed enthusiasm of a mere lover of nature." As in the case of many other subjects, Thoreau's view of nature was replete with paradox. Passionately eager to see, to know, to understand, he nevertheless feared that in looking too closely, in knowing too many facts, the vision and the poetry would be lost. Deeply read in oriental philosophy, he cherished his sudden moments of illumination.

Unlike Emerson, Thoreau yearned for wildness, for "a nature I cannot put my foot through." Unable to experience the vast wilderness of the American West, he had made the most of his trips to Mount Monadnock and New Hampshire's White Mountains. And finally, only a month after his night in the Concord jail, he seized the opportunity for his first journey to the true wilderness. A cousin in the lumber business in Bangor, Maine, who wanted to inspect some property on the West Branch of the Penobscot River—and who was aware of Henry's interest in the forest and the Indians—invited him to come along. On August 31, 1846, Thoreau set out by rail and steamer to Bangor, by stagecoach to road's end, and thence—with local guides—upriver by bateau to the chain of lakes leading toward Mount Ktaadn*, which Henry was determined to climb. "Some hours only of travel," he commented, "will carry the curious to the verge of a primitive forest, more interesting, perhaps . . . than they would reach by going a thousand miles westward."

The first part of the trip was not reassuring, with its huge sawmills and logjams in the river, where the "once green tree . . . becomes lumber merely. . . . The mission of men there seems to be, like so many busy demons, to drive the forest all out of the country . . . as soon as possible." As today one contemplates the destruction of California's ancient redwoods, so Henry thought of a great white pine in the Maine woods, "its boughs soughing with the four winds, and every individual needle trembling in the sunlight—sold, perchance, to the New England Friction-Match Company!" But he cheered up as they continued upstream in the bateau, using iron-tipped spruce poles, and "shot up the rapids like a salmon. . . . I, who had had some experience in boating, had never experienced any[thing] half so exhilarating before." Soon he felt that they were in truly wild country, where the howl of

*Indian for "highest land"; now spelled *Katahdin*.

wolves (though they had yet to hear it) "was a common serenade" and where an "utterly uncivilized, big-throated owl hooted loud and dismally in the drear and boughy wilderness."

When at length a high camp had been made on the slopes of the mountain itself, Henry went on alone, scrambling up over huge rocks toward a summit hidden by heavy mist. "Occasionally, when the windy columns broke in on me, I caught sight of a dark, damp crag to the right or left," he noted. The scene "was vast, Titanic, and such as man never inhabits. Some part of the beholder . . . seems to escape through the loose grating of his ribs as he ascends." Here "inhuman Nature" had man at a disadvantage: "She seems to say sternly 'Why came ye here before your time. Is it not enough that I smile in the valleys.' " As Thoreau fought his way up to the tableland of the summit, he was in another world—a world apart from the gentle landscape of the Sudbury and Concord valley, where he could find true wilderness only within himself.

Thoreau rejected the biblical assumption that the world was created for the use of human beings. It is beautiful, but it is also savage and awful: "I looked with awe at the ground I trod on . . . , here was no man's garden . . . not lawn, nor pasture, nor mead, nor woodland . . . nor waste-land." Anticipating a phrase made familiar by today's environmentalists, he referred to the fresh and natural surface of "the planet Earth." "So Nature made it, and man may use it if he can." Here on the windswept summit he seems to have achieved a heightened sense of awareness, almost of ecstasy: "Talk of mysteries! Think of our life in nature,—daily to be shown matter, to come in contact with it,—rocks, trees, wind on our cheeks! The *solid* earth! The *actual* world! The *common sense*! *Contact*! *Contact*! *Who* are we? *Where* are we?"'*

As the year drew to a close, Thoreau was back in Concord, enjoying his second winter on Walden Pond. He liked winter: a landscape stripped bare, trees etched in sharp silhouette against the sky. Now the sound of the woodchopper's ax, the distant clarion of the cock, came clear and bell-like through the frosty air. "The wonderful purity of nature at this season is a most pleasing fact," Henry wrote of a winter walk. "A cold and searching wind drives away all contagion." No false notes, no soft edges, no compromise. On his daily excursions he would pause occasionally to make brief, cryptic jottings in his homemade pocket notebook, holding the paper tight against the wind. Later he would add "the most significant and poetic part. I do not know at first what charms me." But as he noted in his journal for that December, "No method or discipline can supersede the necessity of being forever on the alert"—one of the many entries that would appear, word for word, in *Walden*.

In Thoreau's world it was always morning. He well knew that a fresh understanding of wild nature, like the recent discoveries of the natural scientists, would raise disturbing questions about man's place in the universe. Whatever the answers, it was now necessary to look at the world with new eyes.

*One thinks of the famous title of Paul Gauguin's last great painting: *D'ou venons nous? Que sommes-nous? ou allons-nous?*

SOURCES

(Unless otherwise noted, all references to Thoreau's *Journal* are from the Princeton edition.)

CHAPTER I, THE TIME, THE PEOPLE, AND THE PLACE

3 R. W. Emerson, *Historical Discourse*, 29–30.
5 William H. Prescott, 1840, *Correspondence* (quoted in Van Wyck Brooks, *The Flowering of New England*, 172n).
6 Vernon L. Parrington, *Main Currents in American Thought*, 382.
7N Edward W. Emerson, *The Early Years of the Saturday Club*, 3.
9 Henty Seidel Canby, *Thoreau*, 186.
9 Henry D. Thoreau, *Walking*.
10 Henry D. Thoreau, *Journal* (Walden edition), vol. 3, 275; vol. 2, 374; vol. 9, 49.
12 *Concord Freeman*, 1846.

CHAPTER II, WALDO AND LIDIAN

18 Ralph Waldo Emerson, *Journal*, November 15, 1834.
18 Oliver Wendell Holmes, *Ralph Waldo Emerson*, 115.
18 *Early Letters of George Wm. Curtis to John S. Dwight*, 14.
19 Ralph L. Rusk, *The Life of Ralph Waldo Emerson*, 307.
19 Ralph L. Rusk, ed., *The Letters of Ralph Waldo Emerson*, January 1846.
20 Bliss Perry, *Emerson Today*, 47.
20 John Albee, *Remembrances of Emerson*, 12.

20 Edith Emerson Webster Gregg, *Emerson and His Children*, Harvard Library Bulletin 28, no. 4 (October 1980).
21 Rusk, *Life*, 230.
22 Mary Hosmer Brown, *Memories of Concord*, 35.
22 Ellen Tucker Emerson, *The Life of Lidian Jackson Emerson*, 95, 104–5.
23 Ibid., 97–98.
25 Edward Waldo Emerson, *Emerson in Concord*, 155, 157.
26 Walter Harding, *The Days of Henry Thoreau*, 225, 227.

CHAPTER III, HILLSIDE AND WALDEN POND

31 Annie Sawyer Downs, *American Heritage* 30, no. 1 (December 1978): 103
32 Henry D. Thoreau, *Journal* (Walden edition), vol. 13, 230.
32 Edward W. Emerson, *Thoreau as Remembered by a Young Friend*, 129.
32 Downs, 97.
33 Madelon Bedell, *The Alcotts*, 150, 234–35.
33 Odell Shepard, *Pedlar's Progress*, 387.
33–34 Bronson Alcott, *Journals*, January 3, 1846.
35 Louisa May Alcott in *Woman's Journal* (quoted in Harding, 228).
35 Bronson Alcott to Samuel May, in Shepard, 389.
35 Bedell, 234, 236.
36 Martha Saxton, *Louisa May*, 153, 155.
38 Bedell, 239.
38 Clara Gowing (quoted in Bedell, 237).
39 Paul Brooks, *Thoreau Country*, introduction.
40–42 Henry D. Thoreau, *Journal* (Princeton edition), vol. 2, 133, 191, 236, 136, 227, 132–33, 147.
42 *Walden*, chapter 6, "Visitors."
42 Mary Hosmer Brown, *Memories of Concord*, 198.
42 George Keyes, quoted by Edward Emerson, *Notes on Thoreau* (Harding, 194.)
42 Frederick L. H. Willis, *Alcott Memoirs* (Bedell, 266).

CHAPTER IV, FRIENDS AND NEIGHBORS

47 Marc Harris, in *Concord: The Social History of a New England Town, 1750–1850*, ed. D. H. Fischer.

47 R. W. Emerson, *Journals*, vol. 7, 162.
47 R. W. Emerson, *Historical Discourse*, 49.
48 Concord town meeting, March 2, 1846.
48 George Frisbie Hoar, *Autobiography of Seventy Years.*
49 George Frisbie Hoar, *Centennial of the Social Circle of Concord*, 2, 14.
49 R. W. Emerson, *Journals*, vol. 8, 156.
50 Robert A. Gross, *New Perspectives on Concord History.*
51 John S. Keyes, ed., *Memoirs of Members of the Social Circle of Concord*, vol. 3, 34, 36.
51 R. W. Emerson, *Biographical Sketches*, 445.
52 *Social Circle Memoirs*, vol. 4, 8, 26, 28.
52 Ibid., 134
55 E. W. Emerson, *Emerson in Concord*, 150.
56 *Social Circle Memoirs*, vol. 4, 143.
56 Henry D. Thoreau, *Journal* (Walden edition), vol. 10, 221.
56 R. W. Emerson, *Journals*, vol. 5, 195.
57 Horace Hosmer, *Remembrances of Concord and the Thoreaus*, 3, 10, 84, 131, 14.
59 Henry D. Thoreau, *Journal*, 1846, 150.
Annie Sawyer Downs, *Memoirs*, 99.

CHAPTER V, THE "ROARING FORTIES"

63–67 *Concord Freeman*, January 2 and 20, 1846.
65–72 Bernard DeVoto, *The Year of Decision, 1846*, 6, 37, 40, 224.
69 R. W. Emerson, *Journals*, vol. 7, 206.
69 Samuel Eliot Morison, *The Oxford History of the American People*, 561.
69 Bragdon, McCutchen, and Cole, *History of a Free People*, 313.
70 Robert W. Johannsen, *To the Halls of Montezuma*, 277, 278.
70 Emerson, 206
DeVoto, 10.
70 Johannsen, 68.
72 DeVoto, 496.

CHAPTER VI, ANTISLAVERY

75–76 DeVoto, 11. Rusk, 227. Harding, 74.
76 *Concord Freeman*, August 7, 1846.

77 Samuel A. Jones: *Thoreau's Incarceration (as Told by His Jailer)*, Thoreau Society Bulletin, no. 4.
Edward W. Emerson: *Thoreau as Remembered by a Young Friend*, 64.
78 Henry D. Thoreau, *Civil Disobedience*, 377.
79 Bronson Alcott, *Journals*, July 25, 1846.
79 R. W. Emerson, *Journals*, vol. 7, 219.
80 Henry D. Thoreau, *Journal*, 262–63.
80–81 Henry D. Thoreau, *Civil Disobedience*, 377, 369.
80n Minutes, Concord Lyceum, Lincoln Lyceum.
81 R. W. Emerson, *Journals*, vol. 7, 201.

CHAPTER VII, BROOK FARM: CONCORD'S UTOPIAN NEIGHBOR

87 S. E. Morison, *Oxford History of the American People*, 524.
88 Edith R. Curtis, *A Season in Utopia*, 22, 37.
89 Ibid.
89 Kenneth R. Cameron, *The Transcendentalists and Minerva*, 816.
89 John T. Codman, *Brook Farm*, 20, 25.
90 Ibid, 75
90 Nathaniel Hawthorne to Sophia Peabody (quoted in James R. Mellow, *Nathaniel Hawthorne in his Times*, 189).
91 Edith R. Curtis, 87, 66, 53.
Lindsay Swift, *Brook Farm*, 88.
91 Codman, 10.
92 George William Curtis, *Early Letters to John S. Dwight*, 222.
93 Edith R. Curtis, 226.
94–96 James W. Mathews, *George Parker Bradford: Friend of Transcendentalists*.
97 Mary Hosmer Brown, *Memories of Concord*, 25.

CHAPTER VIII, THE CONCORD FARMER

101 F. O. Matthiessen, *American Renaissance,* 632.
102 *Social Circle Memoirs*, vol. 3, 98–99.
102–5 Josephine L. Swayne, *The Story of Concord.*
102 Lindsay Swift, *Brook Farm*, 89.
105 Edward W. Emerson, *Emerson in Concord*, 137.
105 R. W. Emerson, *Journals*, vol. 4, 203.

106 Henry D. Thoreau, *Journal* (Walden edition), vol. 8, 194.
110 Brian Donahue, in *Concord: The Social History of a New England Town, 1750–1850*, ed. D. H. Fischer, 32.
111 John F. Wilinsky: *The Impact of the Railroad on Concord, Massachusetts.*
112 *Citizens' Petition Concerning Impact of the Railroad on Concord.* Concord Public Library.
112 Henry D. Thoreau, *Journal.*
114 *Social Circle Memoirs,* vol. 4, 180–83 (Edward Carver Damon).

CHAPTER IX, INSTRUCTION: SUNDAYS AND WEEKDAYS

119 Conrad Wright, "Emerson, Barzillai Frost, and the Divinity School Address," *Harvard Theological Review* 49, no. 1 (January 1955).
120–21 Dana McLean Greeley, "The Church and Its Ministers," in *The Meeting House on the Green*, Concord, 1985, 22.
121 Grinnell Reynolds, "Addison Grant Fay," in *Social Circle Memoirs*, vol. 3, 84.
123 Morton R. Seavey, *Concord Schools: From Candles to Kerosene.*
123 Merle Curti, *The Growth of American Thought*, 360–61.
124–26 Susan Walton, *A Process of Acculturation.*
123 Report of the school committee, 1846.
127 John Albee, *Remembrances of Emerson*, 32.
127–29 R. W. Emerson, *Journals*, vol. 7, 166, 226.
128–29 R. W. Emerson, *Letters*, 335.
130 Merle Curti, *The Growth of American Thought*, 366.
132 W. L. Schroeder, *Oliver Wendell Holmes: An Appreciation.*
132 William Ellery Sedgwick, *Herman Melville: The Tragedy of Mind.*
133 Herman Melville to Evert Duychinck, March 3, 1849.
133 John Albee, *Remembrances of Emerson*, 12.
133 Mary Hosmer Brown, *Memories of Concord*, 45.

CHAPTER X, THE LITERARY SCENE

137–38 James R. Mellow, *Nathaniel Hawthorne in His Times*, 265, 250.
140 R. W. Emerson, *Journals*, vol. 7, 188.
140 Henry D. Thoreau, *Journal*, 1846, 265.
140–41 Walter Harding, *The Days of Henry Thoreau*, 188, 243.
143 R. W. Emerson, *Letters* (ed. Ralph L. Rusk), February 16, 1846, 326.
143 Mellow, 213.
143 Paula Blanchard, *Margaret Fuller*, 209.
144 R. W. Emerson, *Letters*, 341.
145–46 Longfellow to Emerson, December 27, 1846.
146 George Tolman, *Mary Moody Emerson*, 28.

CHAPTER XI, WHAT THEY WERE READING

151 J. S. Goldberg, *The Library in America.*
152 Edward Jarvis, "Traditions and Reminiscences of Concord, 1779–1886." (Unpublished manuscript, Concord Public Library.)
152 *Social Circle Memoirs*, vol. 3, 37.
153 *Literary History of the United States*, bibliography, 115.
153 Frank Luther Mott, *Golden Multitudes*, 134.
154 *Literary History of the United States*, bibliography, 126.
154 Mott, *Golden Multitudes*, 81.
154 Ibid. 83, 82.
155 John McAleer, *Ralph Waldo Emerson*, 549, 548.
155 Oliver Wendell Holmes, *The Poet at the Breakfast Table.*
157 Mott, *A History of American Magazines.*
158 Ibid. 580–582.
159 James R. Mellow, *Nathaniel Hawthorne in His Times*, 228, 282.
159–160 Ralph L. Rusk, *The Life of Ralph Waldo Emerson*, 305, 405, 309.

CHAPTER XII, SARAH AND ELIZABETH

163 Gamaliel Bradford, *Portraits of American Women*, 36.
164 Elizabeth Hoar, "Life of Mrs. Samuel Ripley," in *Worthy Women of Our First Century.*

165 John McAleer, *Ralph Waldo Emerson*, 47.
166 James B. Thayer, "The Rev. Samuel Ripley of Waltham," (prepared for the Social Circle of Concord).
167 Bradford, 35.
169 G. F. Hoar, *Autobiography of Seventy Years*, vol. 1, 60.
169 E. W. Emerson, *Emerson in Concord*, 119.
170 Elizabeth Maxfield-Miller, *Elizabeth of Concord*, 291.
172 Ibid. 232, 254.
172 James R. Mellow, *Nathaniel Hawthorne in His Times*, 210.
172 G. W. Curtis, *Early Letters to John S. Dwight*, 250.
173 Elizabeth Hoar to R. W. Emerson; *Elizabeth of Concord*, 146.

CHAPTER XIII, WOMEN IN A MAN'S WORLD

177–79 Eleanor Flexner, *Century of Struggle*, 32, 33, 26.
179 R. W. Emerson, *Representative Men* (Harvard Edition), 26.
179 R. W. Emerson, *Journals*, vol. 6, 134.
179 R. W. Emerson, *Letters*, vol. 4, 230.
180 Henry D. Thoreau, *Journal*, (Walden edition), vol. 4, 114.
180–81 Henry D. Thoreau, *Journal*, vol. 2, 244.
181 Madelon Bedell, *The Alcotts*, 128.
181 Abby Alcott, *Journal*, August 26, 1843.
183 James R. Mellow, *Nathaniel Hawthorne in His Times*, 205.
183 Ellen Tucker Emerson, *Life of Lidian Jackson Emerson*, xvii.
183 Mellow, *Hawthorne*, 135.
183–84 R. W. Emerson to Frederic Henry Hodge, November 7, 1846.
184 Mellow, *Hawthorne*, 392, 395.
184 Bedell, *The Alcotts*, 128–29.
184 Bronson Alcott, *Letters*.
185 Blanchard, *Margaret Fuller*, 140.
186 Bell Gale Chevigny, *The Woman and the Myth*, 184.
186 Margaret Fuller, *Essays*.
186 Ibid.
187 Elizabeth Cody Stanton and Susan B. Anthony, *The History of Women's Suffrage*, vol. 1, 801.

CHAPTER XIV, SEEING THE WORLD WITH NEW EYES

191 Bernard DeVoto, *The Year of Decision, 1846*, 217.
192 Merle Curti, *The Growth of American Thought*, 310.
192 R. W. Emerson, *Journals*, vol. 7, 100.
191–92 Ibid., 52.
194 Barbara Novak, *Nature and Culture*, 56, 62.
194 A. Hunter Dupree, *Asa Gray*, 151, 145.
195 R. W. Emerson, *Journals*, vol. 7, 211.
195 R. W. Emerson, *Nature*.
197–98 Nathaniel Hawthorne, *Mosses from an Old Manse*.
199 Henry D. Thoreau, Ktaadn (in *The Maine Woods*).
201 Henry D. Thoreau, *Journal*, 357.

BIBLIOGRAPHY

Albee, John. *Remembrances of Emerson*. New York, 1901.

Alcott, Amos Bronson. *The Journals of Bronson Alcott*. Edited by Odell Shepard. Boston, 1938.

———. *Letters of Amos Bronson Alcott*. Edited by Richard L. Herrnstadt. Ames, Iowa, 1969.

———. *Ralph Waldo Emerson: An Estimate of his Character and Genius*. Boston, 1882.

Bedell, Madelon. *The Alcotts: Biography of a Family*. New York, 1980.

Blanchard, Paula. *Margaret Fuller: From Transcendentalism to Revolution*. Boston, 1978.

Bradford, Gamaliel. "Sarah Alden Ripley." In *Portraits of American Women*. Boston, 1919.

Brooks, Paul. *The Old Manse and the People Who Lived There*. Beverly, Mass.: The Trustees of Reservations, 1983.

Brooks, Van Wyck. *The Flowering of New England*. New York, 1936.

Brown, Mary Hosmer. *Memories of Concord*. Boston, 1926.

Barton, Katherine. *Paradise Planters: The Story of Brook Farm*. New York, 1939.

Cameron, Kenneth Walter. *The Transcendentalists and Minerva*. Hartford, 1958.

Canby, Henry Seidel. *Thoreau*. Boston, 1939.

Channing, William Ellery. *Thoreau: The Poet-Naturalist*. Boston, 1902.

Chevigny, Bell Gale. *The Woman and the Myth: Margaret Fuller's Life and Writings*. New York, 1976.

"Citizens' Petition concerning Impact of the Railroad on Concord." Concord, Mass.: Concord Public Library.

Codman, John Thomas. *Brook Farm: Historic and Personal Memoirs*. Boston, 1894.

Concord Freeman. 1846.

Concord Lyceum. "Minutes." 1846.

Curti, Merle. *The Growth of American Thought*. New York, 1943.

Curtis, Edith Roelker. *A Season in Utopia: The Story of Brook Farm*. New York, 1961.

Curtis, George William. *Early Letters of George Wm. Curtis to John S. Dwight: Brook Farm and Concord*. Edited by George Willis Cooke. New York, 1898.

DeVoto, Bernard. *The Year of Decision: 1846*. Boston, 1943.

Downs, Annie Sawyer. "Memoirs." Edited by Walter Harding. *American Heritage* 30, no. 1 (December 1978).

Dupree, A. Hunter. *Asa Gray*. Cambridge, 1959.

Emerson, Edward Waldo. *The Early Years of the Saturday Club*. Boston, 1918.

———. *Emerson in Concord*. Boston, 1888.

———. *Henry Thoreau as Remembered by a Young Friend*. Boston, 1917.

Emerson, Ellen Tucker. *The Life of Lidian Jackson Emerson*. Edited by Delores Bird Carpenter. Boston, 1980.

Emerson, Ralph Waldo. *Complete Works*. Harvard edition. Boston, 1929.

———. *Journals*. Edited by Edward Waldo Emerson. Boston, 1909.

———. *The Letters of Ralph Waldo Emerson*. Edited by Ralph L. Rusk. New York, 1939.

Fischer, David Hackett, ed. *Concord: The Social History of a New England Town, 1750–1850*. Waltham, Mass.: Brandeis University, 1983.

Flexner, Eleanor. *Century of Struggle: The Women's Rights Movement in the United States*. Cambridge, 1959.

Fuller, Margaret. *Essays on American Life and Letters*. Edited by Joel Myerson. New Haven, 1978.

Garrelick, Renee. *Clothier of the Assabet*. Concord, 1988.

Goldberg, Joselyn Schnier. *The Library in America & the American Reading Public*. Concord Public Library Pamphlet.

Gray, Jane Loring, ed. *Letters of Asa Gray*. Boston, 1893.

Greeley, Dana McLean. "The Church and Its Ministers." In *The Meeting House on the Green*, edited by John W. Teele. Concord, Mass., 1985.

Gregg, Edith Emerson Webster. "Emerson and His Children: Their Childhood Memories." *Harvard Library Bulletin* 28 no. 4 (October 1980).

Gross, Robert A. *Much Instruction from Little Reading: Books and Libraries in Thoreau's Concord*. Pamphlet. Concord, Mass.: Concord Public Library, 1985.

———. *New Perspectives on Concord History: Transcendentalism and Urbanism*. Pamphlet. Concord, Mass.: Concord Public Library, 1982.

Harding, Walter. *The Days of Henry Thoreau*. New York, 1965.

Harris, Mark. "Demographic Study of Concord, 1750–1850." Typescript. Concord, Mass.: Concord Public Library, 1973.

Hawthorne, Nathaniel. *The American Notebooks*. Centenary edition, edited by Claude M. Simpson. Columbus, Ohio, 1972.

———. *Mosses from an Old Manse*. Boston, 1846.

Hoar, Elizabeth. "Life of Mrs. Samuel Ripley." In *Worthy Women of Our First Century*, edited by Wister and Irwin. Philadelphia, 1877.

Hoar, George Frisbie. *Autobiography of Seventy Years*. New York, 1903.

Holmes, Oliver Wendell. *Ralph Waldo Emerson*. Boston, 1885.

Hosmer, Horace. *Remembrances of Concord and the Thoreaus: Letters of Horace Hosmer to Dr. S. A. Jones*. Edited by George Hendrick. Urbana: University of Illinois Press, 1977.

Hosmer, Joseph. "Henry D. Thoreau: Some Recollections and Incidents concerning Him," *Concord Freeman*, 1880. Reprinted in Horace Hosmer, *Remembrances*.

Howe, Irving. *The American Newness*. Cambridge, Mass., 1980.

Jarvis, Edward. "Traditions and Reminiscences of Concord, 1779–1886." Unpublished manuscript. Concord Public Library, Concord, Massachusetts.

Johannsen, Robert W. *To the Halls of Montezuma*. New York, 1985.

Keyes, John S., ed. *The Centennial of the Social Circle in Concord*. Concord, Mass., 1882.

———, ed. *Memoirs of Members of the Social Circle in Concord*. Cambridge, Mass., 1907.

Larkin, Jack. *The Reshaping of Everyday Life: 1790–1840*. New York, 1988.

Larson, Mary. *The Concord Academy: 1822–1862*. Pamphlet. Concord, Mass.: Concord Public Library.

Literary History of the United States. New York, 1948.

Mathews, James W. *George Partridge Bradford: Friend of Transcendentalists*. Pamphlet. Concord, Mass.: Concord Public Library, 1981.

Matthiessen, F. O. *American Renaissance: Art and Expression in the Age of Emerson and Whitman*. New York, 1957.

Maxfield-Miller, Elizabeth. "Elizabeth of Concord: Selected Letters of

Elizabeth Sherman Hoar (1814–1878)." In *Studies in the American Renaissance*. Charlottesville, Va., 1984–86.

McAleer, John. *Ralph Waldo Emerson: Days of Encounter*. Boston, 1984.

Mellow, James R. *Nathaniel Hawthorne in His Times*. Boston, 1980.

Morison, Samuel Eliot. *The Oxford History of The American People*. New York, 1965.

Mott, Frank Luther. *American Journalism: A History, 1690–1960*. New York, 1962.

———. *Golden Multitudes: The Story of Best Sellers in the United States*. New York, 1947.

———. *A History of American Magazines, 1741–1850*. Cambridge, Mass., 1957.

Myerson, Joel, ed. *Margaret Fuller: Essays on American Life and Letters*. New Haven, 1978.

Novak, Barbara. *Nature and Culture: American Landscape and Painting, 1825–1875*. New York, 1980.

Parrington, Vernon Louis. *Main Currents in American Thought*. New York, 1927.

Perry, Bliss. *Emerson Today*. Princeton, N.J., 1931.

Richardson, Robert D., Jr. *Henry Thoreau: A Life of the Mind*. Berkeley, Calif., 1986.

Ripley Family. Pamphlet. Concord, Mass.: Concord Public Library.

Rusk, Ralph L. ed. *Letters of Ralph Waldo Emerson*. New York, 1939.

———. *The Life of Ralph Waldo Emerson*. New York, 1949.

Russell, Phillips. *Emerson: The Wisest American*. New York, 1929.

Sanborn, Frank B. "Emerson and His Friends in Concord." *New England Magazine* 3, no. 4 (December 1890).

Saxton, Martha. *Louisa May: A Modern Biography of Louisa May Alcott*. Boston, 1977.

Schlesinger, Arthur M., Jr. *Orestes A. Brownson: A Pilgrim's Progress*. Boston, 1939.

Scudder, Townsend. *Concord: American Town*. Boston, 1947.

Seavey, Morton R. Concord Schools: from Candles to Kerosene, 1799–1893. Manuscript. Concord Public Library, 1946.

Shepard, Odell. *Pedlar's Progress*. Boston, 1937.

Swayne, Josephine Latham. *The Story of Concord, as Told by Concord Writers*. Boston, 1911.

Swift, Lindsay. *Brook Farm: Its Members, Scholars, and Visitors*. New York, 1900.

Tharp, Louise Hall. *The Peabody Sisters of Salem*. Boston, 1950.

Thoreau, Henry D. *Complete Works: Walden Edition*. Boston, 1906.

———. *Journal*. Edited by Bradford Torrey and Francis H. Allen. Boston, 1906.

———. *Journal: 1842–1848*. Edited by Robert Sattelmeyer. Princeton, 1984.

———. *Men of Concord*. Edited by Francis H. Allen. Boston, 1936.

———. *Walden: or Life in the Woods*. Boston, 1854.

Thoreau Society Bulletin.

Tichnor, Caroline. *Classic Concord*. Boston, 1926.

Tolman, George. *Mary Moody Emerson*. Pamphlet. Concord, Mass.: Concord Public Library, 1929.

Town of Concord. "Minutes of Town Meetings." "Report of the Town Treasurer." "Report of the School Committee." "Town Census: 1840, 1850."

Voye, Nancy. "Marriage in Concord, 1845–1855." Typescript. Concord, Mass.: Concord Public Library.

Wade, Mason. *Margaret Fuller: Whetstone of Genius*. New York, 1940.

Walton, Susan. *A Process of Acculturation: The Concord Common Schools at Mid-Century*. Pamphlet. Concord, Mass.: Concord Public Library.

Wheeler, Ruth R. *Concord: Climate for Freedom*. Concord, Mass., 1967.

Wilinsky, John F. *The Impact of the Railroad on Concord, Massachusetts*. 1844–1877.

Wright, Conrad. "Emerson, Barzillai Frost, and the Divinity School Address." *The Harvard Theological Review* 59, no. 1 (January 1955).

INDEX

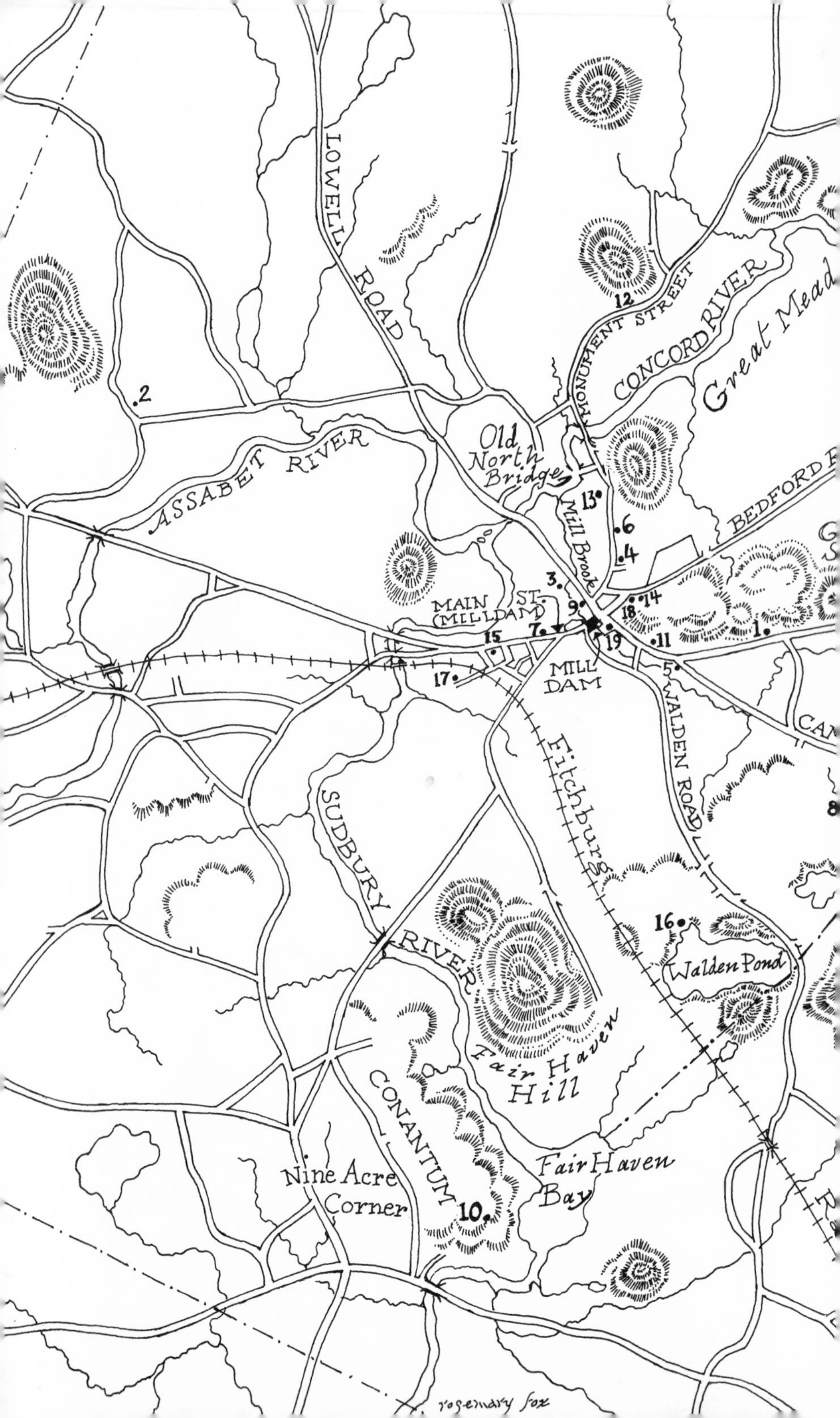
LOWELL ROAD
MONUMENT STREET
CONCORD RIVER
Great Mead
12
.2
ASSABET RIVER
Old North Bridge
13
Mill Brook
.6
.4
BEDFORD
3.
MAIN ST. (MILLDAM)
9
18
14
15
7.
19
11
1.
17
MILL DAM
5
WALDEN ROAD
CA
Fitchburg
SUDBURY RIVER
8
16
Walden Pond
Fair Haven Hill
CONANTUM
Nine Acre Corner
Fair Haven Bay
10.
rosemary fox